HALF JAPANESE

Japanese Children of Visibly Mixed Ethnic and Cultural Heritage

By:
Timothy Dooley

DEDICATION

For Taiga & Mei

CONTENTS

Acknowledgements

I wish to sincerely thank the families that participated; their honesty and insights are the heart of this book.

PREFACE

Japan is a country with a long history, distinct traditions, and is rich in social and cultural imagery. Even for those who have never read about or visited Japan the words samurai, sumo, and sushi come to mind and evoke feelings of things quintessentially Japanese. From cars to electronics, anime to video games, cherry blossoms to geisha, Japan has an abundance of popular images. These are some of the positive iconic symbols that people associate with Japan and are in many ways the pretty wrapping that Japan displays to the outside world.

Japan, however, has a darker side in both its past and present. When we look beyond the surface and the positive imagery we find the negative side of Japanese society in the form of discrimination, power and sexual harassment in the workplace, death from overwork, bullying in schools, high suicide rates, and sexless marriages, being some of these issues.

Japan today is facing some drastic changes in both a literal and physical sense. The main reasons for these changes are a rapidly aging population, a negative birthrate, greater numbers of tourists visiting and immigrants coming to work and live in Japan like never before.

Minority groups and people of different ethnic and cultural backgrounds have always lived in Japan but a new group of visibly mixed ethnic and cultural Japanese people has continued to steadily rise in the last few decades. These Japanese born and raised in Japan are referred to as *hafu* in Japanese as in the English word 'half'. They are the offspring of international marriage between Japanese and foreign parents. Due to the foreign parent's different physical appearance, they also have a different phenotype than the stereotypical 'mainstream' Japanese. But as they are born and raised in Japan they have native language and cultural fluency. These biracial Japanese by their very existence alone have questioned ideas of Japanese homogeneity and furthered the dialogue about what it means to be Japanese today.

This book will look at multicultural families with Japanese children of visibly mixed ethnic and cultural heritage living in Japan. In particular, it will look at the parental strategies used in raising their children in Japan. Through interviews with these families, a personal perspective on the challenges of raising a biracial Japanese child in a multicultural family in Japan will be explored. By looking at the literature and research that exists on mixed ethnic and cultural Japanese living in Japan and by examining Japanese society in the present and from a historical perspective a deeper understanding of what it means to be considered and treated like an 'outsider' in Japan will be seen.

In the last few decades, increasing numbers of biracial Japanese have been born, raised, and live in Japan. From everyday walks of life to the boom of celebrity *hafus* now seen on Japanese TV the face of Japan has changed and will continue to change. Outside of Japan on the world stage, more and more Japanese of visibly mixed ethnic cultural heritage are also creating a buzz in the media. Naomi Osaka, won the 2018 US tennis Open, has a Haitian father and a Japanese mother. Yu Darvish, plays major league baseball in the USA, has an Iranian father and a Japanese mother. Sakai Gotoku, captain of his German Bundesliga soccer team, has a German mother and Japanese father. Ariana Miyamoto, Miss Universe Japan 2015, has an African-American father and Japanese mother. These are some of the higher profile figures that were either born, raised or living in Japan that are asking the question of what it means to be Japanese in both a cultural and physical sense.

1. INTRODUCTION

The two main discourses about Japanese ethnicity and culture are the homogeneous Japan and multicultural Japan discourses. The homogeneous Japan discourse depicts Japanese society as being monoethnic, monoracial, monocultural and monolingual. The multicultural Japan discourse points to the various native Japanese minority and foreign groups that exist and argues that Japanese society is multiethnic, multiracial, multicultural and multilingual. The multicultural Japan discourse can give the impression that majority 'mainstream' Japanese and 'outsider' minority and foreign groups are distinct ethnic and cultural groups that exist in isolation from each other (Burgess, 2004, 2007, 2010; Murphy-Shigematsu, 2008; Okano and Tsuneyoshi, 2011).

This book is about a minority group in Japan that blurs the common distinctive and distinguishable representations of 'insider' and 'outsider' of Japanese and foreigner, *nihonjin* and *gaijin*, as it is on the children of international marriage between 'mainstream' Japanese and non-Asian foreigners. These Japanese children of mixed ethnic and cultural heritage are commonly referred to as *hafus* in Japan and are a minority group that is increasing in number. In this introduction, I will show why this minority group will continue to increase and how Japan is changing demographically and why it is in need of change.

The changes Japan will experience will largely be a result of its declining birthrate and aging population. Many countries in the world will experience similar demographic changes but Japan is near the top or the leader in many areas. The effects of Japan's diminishing population due to a decline in births, coupled with a decreasing working-age population and an increasing elderly population who are living longer, will have far-reaching effects on all aspects of society. The effects will not only be social and economic but political and cultural too. The most obvious but contentious solution would be to allow more foreign workers into Japan.

Japan's Changing Demographic Structure

Japan's population as of most recent figures is around 126,500,000 people (MIC, 2018a). But due to its declining birthrate is expected to see steady and significant declines with future medium-range fertility and mortality projections pointing to the 2050 population being around 100 million. The main concern for Japan in the future is the ratio of the various age groups within the population. By 2050 there will be greater numbers of elderly supported by fewer workers and fewer children being born to fill the jobs than there has been in the past (see Figure 1). It has been estimated that in 2050 an average of 1.3 workers will be financially supporting a senior citizen (Kaneko, et al., 2008).

Japan, due to its dramatic demographic shift, may come to be known as the land of the setting sun. The present median age in the world is 29.6 years old but in Japan, it is 46.3 which is the oldest median age in the world (UN, 2017). Japan is also the present leader in life expectancy with an average longevity of 84 years (MIC, 2015). By 2050 it has been estimated that the median age in the world will be 38 but in Japan, it will be about 55 and 40% of the population will be over 60 years old. At the moment Japan is one of the countries with the highest percentage of population aged 80 and older and will continue to be as of mid-century at which time it will also be the leader in centenarians when it is expected that 800,000 people will be 100 years of age or older (UN, 2010). The ramifications of this sharp rise in aged persons, referred to as hyper-aging, will be particularly challenging to Japan because much of its population will be very old and dependent on others for care. As the United Nations has pointed out:

> Population ageing is profound, having major consequences and implications for all facets of human life. In the economic area, population ageing will have an impact on economic growth, savings, investment, consumption, labour markets, pensions, taxation and intergenerational transfers. In the social sphere, population ageing influences family composition and living arrangements, housing demand, migration trends, epidemiology and the need for healthcare services. In the political arena, population ageing may shape voting patterns and political representation (UN, 2010: xxv).

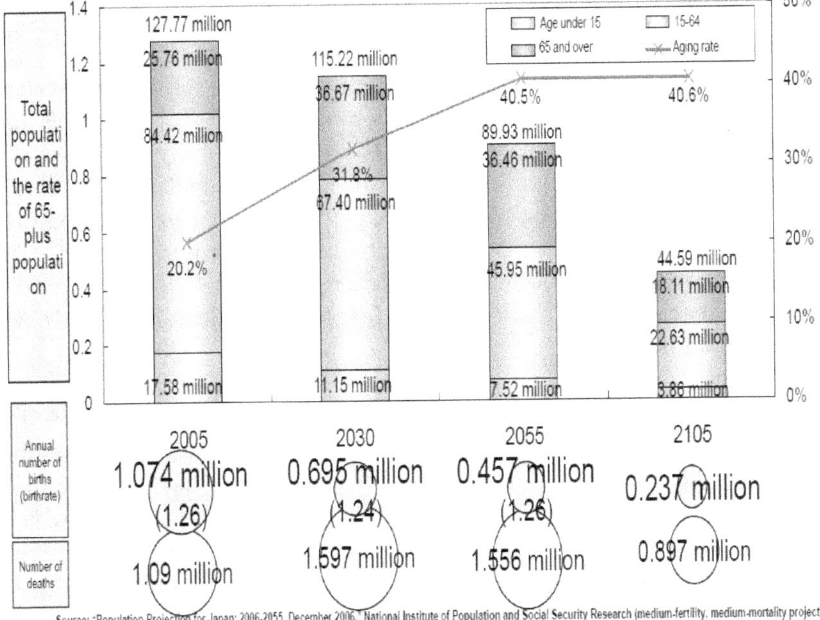

Compounding Japan's aging population crisis is the declining birth rate (see Figure 2). Japan experienced its lowest recorded birthrate per woman in 1989 and the phrase "1.57 Shock" was used to describe the low figure. In 1994 the government initiated the "The Angel Plan" to encourage more births by Japanese couples but it was unsuccessful (Haub, 2010). In 1997 the Japanese Ministry of Health Labor and Welfare published a report about the continuing trends of a decreasing population and of Japanese having fewer children. It gave some grave predictions of what the future might hold:

It is envisioned that the impending decrease in population is much more threatening to our society than assumed in the past… we must carry out drastic reforms of the economy, social security system, government finance system and others. In the face of this challenge, we cannot afford to be optimistic, however, about the future of a society with a decreasing population even if we are successful in implementing these structural reforms (MHLW, 1997 Section I).

Japan is now many years removed from the issue of this report but government reforms have had little effect on the birthrate which reached a new low of 1.26 births per woman in 2005. In 2009 a "New Angel Plan" failed in its promise to increase the number of daycares due to financial considerations (Haub, 2010).

The declining birthrate in Japan is one of the highest rates of decline in the developing world and there are no signs that it will significantly change any time soon with future medium-range projections of about 1.25 until 2050 (Kaneko, et al., 2008). A minimum rate of 2.07 is needed to avoid a decline in population (UN, 2009). Japan's birthrate is now around 1.43 but the number of children in Japan (0-14 years old) has fallen for 37 consecutive years and the ratio of children to the total population has hit its lowest point of 12.3% in its 44 consecutive year slide. Another ominous statistic is that the mortality rate has been higher than the fertility rate for 11 consecutive years in the declining population trend (MIC, 2018). In 2016 annual births fell below 1 million for the first time since 1899 statistics have been recorded (NPC, 2017).

Japanese government programs and subsidies to support working mothers with children is considered insufficient and another factor in the low birthrate (Goodman and Harper, 2007). A major reason cited for the failure of these programs was the lack of funding which paled in comparison to the funding of senior-citizen backed programs in which "70% of the social-welfare budget goes to programs for the aged, such as pensions and medical services, with only 4% set aside for children, such as child benefits and child-care services" (Hisane, 2006:2).

In 2016 an anonymous social media post brought unexpected attention to the issue. Someone claiming to be a mother wrote that she might have to quit her job because of the lack of child-care facilities. The post titled: "I couldn't get day care – die Japan!!!" received support on social media where it was shared 50,000 times. The initial dismissive response to the post by Prime Minister Shinzo Abe led to government criticism on social media, a protest outside of the Diet parliament building and a petition for change signed by 30,000 people (Nonomiya and Oda, 2016).

Another reason fertility is so low in Japan is that Japanese are marrying less and later in life and the number of extramarital births in Japan at about 1% is extremely low when compared to other industrialized countries, where the average extramarital births in 62 countries polled by the United Nations was 29.2% (2010a). Even if there was a sudden dramatic increase in the birth rate there would still be a "dangerous twenty year gap before a new workforce" emerged (Clark, 2005:1). A sudden population spike, however, seems unlikely because Japan has the highest rate of 'sexless' marriages in the world (Arudou, 2011) and more than 40% of Japanese adults between the ages of 18 and 34 are virgins (CNN, 2018).

Fig.2

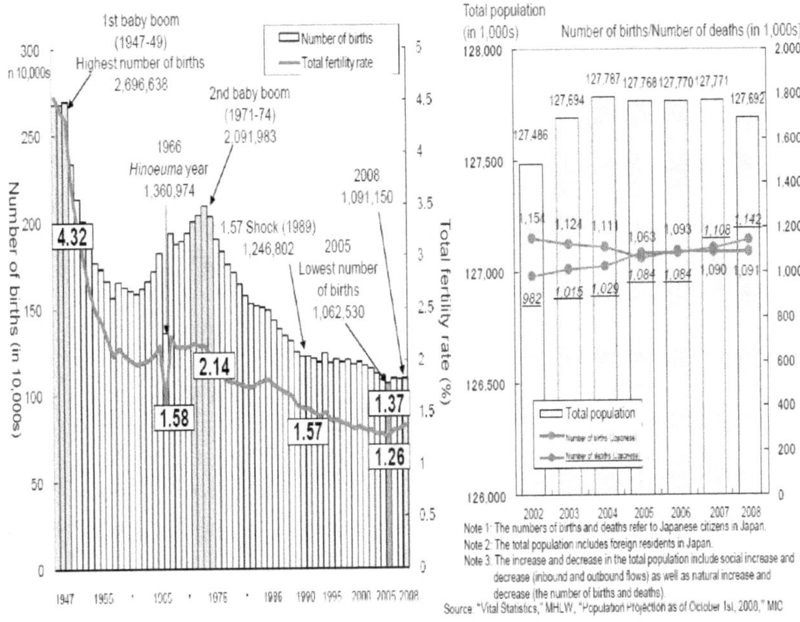

Foreign Workers and Immigration in Japan

The most obvious way to relieve the various stresses on Japan would be to allow more foreign workers into Japan to help fill the ranks of the dwindling Japanese workforce. In 2000 it was estimated by the Japanese government that Japan would need to bring in 600,000 immigrants a year to sustain its workforce, standard of living and current tax level (Arudou, 2007). By 2030 it is estimated that 1 in 20 people will need to be employed in the nursing industry alone to provide the current level of health-care (Hisane, 2006). In 2008 a group of Japanese lawmakers from the Liberal Democratic Party suggested that the foreign population should increase to 10% by 2050 (McNeill, et al., 2009). There are a variety of estimates for the needed number of foreign workers and immigration levels. These demographic projections take into account future socio-economic consequences for Japan given low, medium and high rates of fertility and mortality (Sakanaka, 2005).

The feasibility and practicality of allowing immigrant workers into Japan on a large scale is a question open to some debate but the necessity and inevitability that immigrants in great numbers are needed and will come to Japan is not. They will be needed for Japan's manufacturing, farming and health industries which cannot survive in its present state without an influx of foreign workers. They would also help internal consumption of goods and services and help pay taxes and support the old age pension system both of which cannot continue as is without a serious strain on the working population's standard of living (Sakanaka, 2005).

Beyond Japan's internal needs the pull of developed countries like Japan will draw immigrants either legally or illegally in search of job opportunities and a better life. Unlike Japan, the world's population is increasing and is presently around 6.8 billion people and is expected to increase to over 9 billion by 2050. The majority of this increase in world population will come from economically under-developed countries (UN, 2009). Japan being one of the most highly developed countries in the world with the third largest economy will no doubt be a destination for many migrant workers.

It seems, however, that Japanese government officials and the general population have been unwilling to let any significant numbers of foreign workers into the country. Some of the main reasons why are the fear of crime, reduced job opportunities, lower salaries for Japanese workers and the general discord that could arise (Clark, 2005; Sakanaka, 2005; Hisane, 2006). Former Prime Minister Koizumi no doubt echoed popular opinion in 2005 when he said, "If [the foreign labor] exceeds a certain level, it is bound to cause a clash. It is necessary to consider measures to prevent it and then admit foreign workers as necessary" (cited in Kashiwazaki, 2006:1).

The Ministry of Justice, which decides immigration policies, is another example of Japanese bureaucracy's general stance on immigrant labor when in a report they concluded that a declining population posed a great threat to the economy but clung to the hope that with better technology, and greater use of the elderly and female population, problems could be solved without resorting to large-scale immigrant labor (Clark, 2005). The popular belief of Japanese homogeneity and xenophobia still lingers in some segments of society and leads to 'mainstream' Japanese being inflexible to immigration and cultural variation:

The native Japanese have lived as a single ethnic group for nearly 1000 years and it will be a difficult task for them to build friendly relationships with other ethnic groups. There will likely be many who would prefer to deal only with other Japanese people rather than foreigners with different customs and ideas (Sakanaka, 2005:7).

Minorities and Foreigners in Japan

It would be an exaggeration to call Japan a multicultural country the likes of Australia, Canada or the U.S.A., which are made up of large populations of visible minority groups but it would also be false to say Japan is a homogeneous culture and society. Local variations of foods, customs and dialects aside, Japan has always had groups of non-Japanese people within its borders (Burgess, 2007). In Japan, minority groups have always lived in or have become a part of Japan through colonization or the expansion of the Japanese Empire or were brought in during periods of war or came through trade. Minority groups have always made up parts of the whole but the image of Japan has really always been and still is that of a very monocultural country with a very homogeneous population. Assimilation into Japanese society rather than the celebration of difference has been Japan's main reaction to ethnic and cultural differences (Weiner, 1997: xiii).

The main minority groups in Japan are the ethnic Ainu and Okinawans who are indigenous to Japan, the Koreans and Chinese who were formerly colonial subjects of the Japanese Empire and the Nikkeijin who are the descendants of Japanese who emigrated to other countries and have returned to Japan. The other main minority group is the non-ethnic native Japanese Burakumin, the descendants of the historical outcaste groups in Japanese society. These main minority groups make up only between 4 to 6% of Japan's population (Roth, 2005).

The majority of registered foreigners in Japan after World War II until 1965 were mainly Korean Nationals who accounted for nearly 90% of the total (MOJ, 2015:5). The majority of these Koreans, and also Chinese, were actually citizens of the Japanese Empire that came to Japan as migrant workers but from 1939 were brought to Japan mainly for forced labor (Yamawaki, 2000:38). They had their right to citizenship taken away from them after the war. They and their offspring who were born in Japan were not entitled to citizenship and were eventually designated as special permanent residents. Many eventually became naturalized Japanese and adopted Japanese names and assimilated into Japanese society.

If naturalized foreigners particularly Koreans and Chinese who are the majority of approximately 400,000 naturalized Japanese who take Japanese citizenship each year were included the number of foreigners would be even larger (Caryl, 2006). In recent years China has passed Korea to become the country with the highest number of registered foreigners in Japan. Today more and more diverse groups of foreigners are making Japan their home but as recent figures show it still less than 2% of the population with 2,121,831 registered foreigners, non-Japanese people on 3 month visas and up, living in Japan (MOJ, 2015:5).

The number of foreigners coming to Japan for tourism and business, including people re-entering, has increased substantially in recent years (see Figure 3). The 2008 global financial crisis and the Great East Japan Earthquake and the ensuing nuclear disaster in Fukushima Prefecture in March 2011, led to temporary slowdowns but figures have steadily risen since and topped 14 million people for the first time in 2014. Over 80% of these new arrivals have come from Asian countries (MOJ, 2015:4). With Tokyo hosting the 2020 Summer Olympics even greater numbers of tourists can be expected in Japan.

The Ministry of Justice recognizes and acknowledges that more foreigners will enter Japan and of the need for foreign labor, business, and tourism to invigorate the economy. This awareness has led to greater acceptance of foreign workers and relaxed visa requirements in recent years (MOJ, 2015:2-9). According to the ministry as of October 2017, "the number of foreign workers in Japan stood at a record 1.28 million, doubling from 680,000 in 2012, with Chinese making up the largest group of around 370,000, followed by Vietnamese and Filipinos" (Kyodo, 2018). The increasing number of foreign workers and tourists has had positive economic benefits for Japan but has also shown Japan's struggles and at times xenophobia in dealing with people of different cultures (Brasor, 2018; Kyodo, 2018).

Fig.3

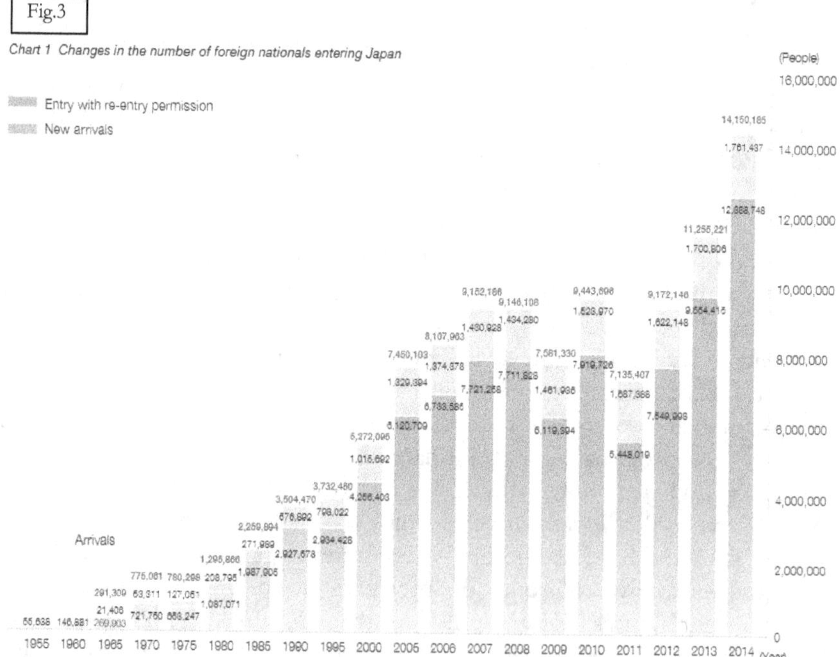

Source: Ministry of Justice (Japan) Basic Plan for Immigration Control 2015 (5th Edition) p.4 <http://immi-moj.go.jp>

International Marriages in Japan

Many foreigners that have and will continue to come to Japan will marry with 'mainstream' Japanese. And while the overall marriage rate in Japan has been decreasing international marriages have been increasing (see Figure 4). As a percentage of total marriages in Japan recent international marriages account for around 5% up from 3.5% of 1995 and 1.5% of 1985 figures. The rate of international marriages in Tokyo is even higher and accounts for 10% of the marriages taking place there (Graburn and Ertl, 2010:21).

Though the trends in international marriage are diverse and many countries are represented the majority consists of women from Asian countries. Foreign women account for the majority of international marriage partners. More than three times that of foreign men. The women come mostly from China, Korea, and the Philippines and the men from Korea, the USA, and China. It is estimated that "more than 75%" of international marriages taking place in Japan are between "Asian and Japanese nationals" meaning that most mixed ethnic and cultural Japanese in Japan are of non-Japanese Asian and 'mainstream' Japanese descent (Lise and Willer, 2009:10).

Mixed Ethnic and Cultural Japanese in Japan

The result of this increase in international marriages is that Japanese children with at least one foreign parent are being born and raised in Japan. Mixed ethnic and cultural Japanese are increasing in number:

One of every 30 babies born in Japan in 2006 had at least one parent originating from overseas, according to a recent government survey. The survey by the Health, Labor and Welfare Ministry found that the mother, father or both parents of 35,651 babies born here originated from countries other than Japan. This represents about 3.2 percent of the 1.1 million babies born nationwide in 2006. The survey indicates that an increasing number of foreign nationals coming to Japan for employment or study are settling in the country, experts said. While the increase in children with at least one non-Japanese parent will broaden the range of cultural background among the country's residents, a lot more needs to be done to accept and provide legal protection for people from different backgrounds, they said. Around 19,000 of the babies had non-Japanese fathers, 26,000 had non-Japanese mothers and 9,000 had parents who were both from abroad, according to the survey (Japan Times, 2008).

Japan is diversifying and these facts will continue to affect the cultural and physical make-up of Japanese people living in Japan. In Tokyo where the highest percentage of international marriages is taking place, it is estimated that "the next generation of school children should be about 25 percent non- or half-Japanese" (Graburn and Ertl, 2010:21). Despite this sharp rise in the number of babies being born into international families, there is very little research being done on these children and their families.

This new minority group consists of a diverse mix of children born of a Japanese parent and a foreign parent that could be from any country in the world. In this sense, this minority group is an eclectic and diverse group that does not necessarily share a language, culture or customs apart from the standard Japanese forms. Therefore, they could be said to be part Japanese and part international, both Japanese and foreign, and depending on the physical features of the foreign parent they may share physical traits of 'mainstream' Japanese. What these children will share above all else is a sense of being different.

Children of mixed cultural heritage are most commonly referred to by Japanese as 'half's' or as Japanese would pronounce it *hafu*. This is a term which elicits various responses ranging from being fashionable and envied for its multicultural connotations to being an almost derogatory term which creates dissonance and separation from the majority 'mainstream' Japanese group.

Lise and Willer (2009) make a distinction between what they call "invisible" and "visible" *hafus*. Invisible *hafus* such as people of mixed Chinese or Korean and Japanese descent "are usually not easily identified or recognized as hafus in society" and it is open to debate "whether Japanese and East Asian individuals self-define as hafus and whether such individuals are considered to be hafus in society". Conversely, visible *hafus* are "imagined to be phenotypically 'different' to 'Japanese people'" (Lise and Willer, 2009:9). The most common and stereotypical image of a *hafu* is a visible *hafu* and usually someone with a 'white' Western English speaking parent and a 'mainstream' Japanese parent (Murphy-Shigematsu, 2001:212; Lise and Willer, 2009:9; Graburn and Ertl, 2010:21; Kamada, 2010:55).

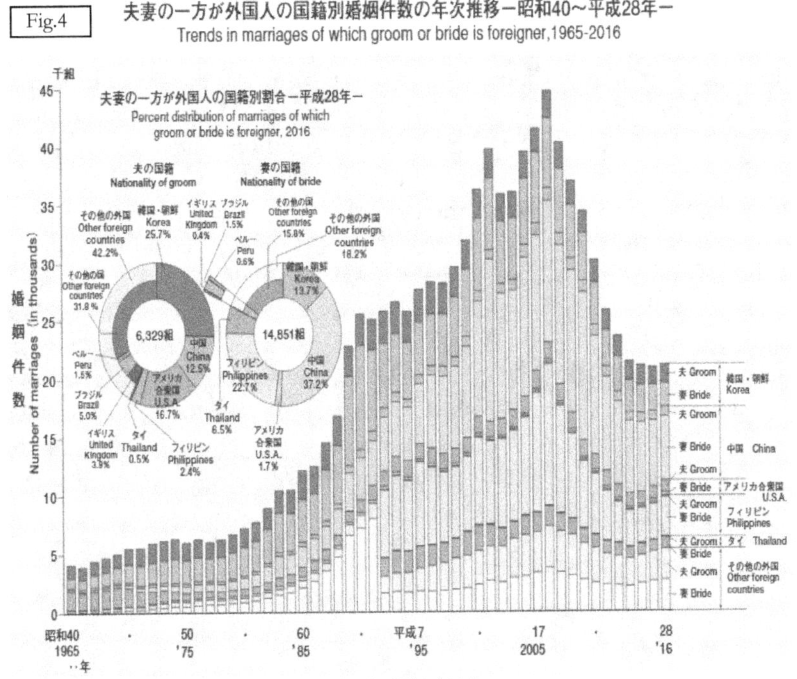

Source: MHLW (Japan) Vital Statistics in Japan (2018) The Latest Trends up to 2016 (p.32) <http://www.mhlw.go.jp/english/>

Outline

This book will focus on Japanese children of visibly mixed ethnic and cultural heritage living in Japan who have a 'white' foreign parent and a 'mainstream' Japanese parent. 'Visible' difference is subjective and culturally constructed but it will be seen that in Japan these children are considered to have a distinguishable and obviously 'different' look from 'mainstream' Japanese.

This group of visibly mixed ethnic and cultural Japanese is enjoying popularity in Japanese mass media and entertainment at the moment but their social status in Japanese society can be marginalized as an 'outsider' *hafu* or even foreigner *gaijin* because they look physically 'different' from 'mainstream' Japanese (Kamada, 2010:32). With further immigration and international marriage the number of Japanese children of mixed ethnic and cultural heritage will continue to increase and their social status, acceptance in Japanese society, as well as their contributions to Japan, will take on greater importance in the future.

The outline of this book is as follows: Chapter one is the introduction to the issues relating to this study. Chapter two is the literary review which introduces research that has been carried out to date on Japanese children of mixed ethnic and cultural heritage living in Japan and the parent's educational strategies. Chapter three is the historical background and looks at how ethnic, cultural and physical difference has been viewed historically in Japan and how this has affected mixed ethnic and cultural Japanese. Chapter four is the methodology and theoretical model and looks at the methods used, intended aims, the participants involved in the study and the research site of the Kawachinagano City in Osaka, Prefecture where most of these families live. Chapter five is the data results chapter which looks in depth at the participant families and details and analyzes the data collected. Chapter six is the discussion chapter and further explores some of the participant's experiences living in Japan and raises some questions about the data collected and discusses other issues relating to Japan. Chapter seven is the conclusion which summarizes the main points of this book.

2. LITERARY REVIEW

This study of Japanese children of visibly mixed ethnic and cultural heritage living in Japan, with a focus on parental educational strategies, is a topic that has not received much attention in the media or academia. The literature on this topic is also limited. What does exist mostly deals with young adults and how they have struggled to come to terms with their mixed ethnic and cultural identity growing up as a minority in Japan. These studies have focused on how the participants have dealt with the multiplicity of their self-identities in the sense of being different in physical appearance and possibly possessing bilingual and bicultural differences from 'mainstream' Japanese.

These are important and interesting issues that create a better understanding of another type of minority in Japan and what it means to be marginalized in Japanese society. However, as the literature up to now has predominantly focused on young adults and their personal experiences growing up in Japan, the parent's educational strategies in regards to choice of schooling, second language learning, cultural transmission, and customs has rarely come up.

Though previous studies have emphasized mixed ethnic and cultural heritage individuals search for identity the importance of parental educational strategies or non-strategies is apparent and inevitably has an effect on their sense of identity. This has especially been seen as the questions about self-identity and place in society increase from adolescence into adulthood (Murphy-Shigematsu, 2000, 2002, 2008; Lise and Willer, 2009; Kamada, 2010).

In this review, I will first look at what has been written on the topic of mixed ethnic and cultural Japanese and briefly summarize these works. I will then summarize the findings from these works as they relate to the themes of schooling, language acquisition, cultural transmission, community-social networks, and names. As this topic has not received much attention I have out of necessity used source material in this review that draws from a variety of disciplines. Some of the literature is academic and some are not and though the focus has not specifically been about parental educational strategies I have read them from the perspective of what insights they could offer on this topic. This literature review was limited by the sparse amount of literature available on the topic and by the fact that only English language sources were consulted.

Source Material

Suzanne Kamata, an American married to a 'mainstream' Japanese with mixed ethnic and cultural twins living in Shikoku Prefecture Japan edited a book, "Call Me Okaasan – Adventures in Multicultural Mothering" in which 20 mothers from around the world offered their perspectives on raising mixed-ethnic and cultural children (Kamata, 2009). The book which is a collection of short autobiographical stories is not academic in focus but still reveals various parental educational strategies. The aim of the book was to give mothers living in foreign countries raising mixed ethnic and cultural children support in dealing with possible identity issues and how to teach their children their native language and culture. A limitation of this work was that only three of the stories take place in Japan and the non-academic style of writing.

Kamada (1995, 1997) interviewed 20 families in Japan that made efforts to raise their children bilingually. These linguistic case studies were the most informative of any of the writings reviewed in regards to parental education strategies for language acquisition. A variety of case studies involving missionary families, Japanese returnee families and mixed cultural families consisting of 'mainstream' Japanese and foreigner were used. Kamada has lived in Japan for many years and is married to a 'mainstream' Japanese partner and they have a mixed ethnic and cultural Japanese son. Unlike the other studies in this review, the focus is on bilingualism and not identity issues. A limitation of this study was the exclusive linguistic focus and that many of the families were not of mixed ethnic and cultural heritage.

Kamada's earlier work which focused on bilingualism gave way to issues of identity in her book, "Hybrid Identities and Adolescent Girls: Being 'Half' in Japan". The study follows the lives of six adolescent girls of mixed ethnic and cultural parentage in which the foreign parents are 'white' native English speaking Westerners from the UK, USA, and Australia, and the other parent is 'mainstream' Japanese (Kamada, 2010). The participant girls live in the Kansai region of Japan in urban areas that have large foreign populations. The study which started in 2001, took place during the girls last year of elementary school in the sixth grade through the three years of junior high school, follows their development by way of interviews and audio recordings in which Kamada focuses on their use of language to gain an understanding of how they negotiate their developing self-identities. The three main questions Kamada wished to explore where the "tensions and dilemmas of hybridity, celebration of hybridity and intersection of hybridity and gender" (Kamada, 2010:11). A major theme of this book which came out in the interviews with the girls is that their physical appearance made them stand out and led to marginalization and feelings of isolation in a Japanese social context.

Kamada, borrowing from Bourdieu's (1977) theory of cultural capital, found that concrete parental educational strategies allowed the girls to develop and construct positive self-identities. Cultural capital and other forms of capital such as linguistic, social and intellectual capital are non-monetary assets that allow for social mobility and status beyond economic means (Grenfell, 2008). Kamada's study is similar to mine in that she has used participants that due to their 'white' foreign parent are visibly distinguishable from 'mainstream' Japanese. A further similarity is that all the participants attend regular Japanese public schools. A limitation of this study was the focus on the girl's use of language without directly looking at parental educational strategies. Another limitation of this study was that only six girls were used as a source of data collection.

"The Hafu Project" by Lise and Willer (2009), like Kamada (2010), also emphasizes the physical appearance of the participants. The interview, research, and photography project deals with Japanese young adults of mixed ethnic and cultural heritage that have grown up both in Japan and abroad, particularly Tokyo and London. The project focused on visibly distinct *hafus* whose parents are 'mainstream' Japanese and a non-Asian foreign parent. The project focused on the physical features of the nine participants using full page close up portrait style photos. The reason given for the emphasis on the physical features of the participants was that it was considered a crucial factor in being considered an 'outsider', especially within Japanese society. Rather than seeking answers the aim of the project was to create a dialogue about the "complexity of culture" (Lise and Willer, 2009:33).

The interviews with the participants gave insights into their stories about growing up as a mixed ethnic and cultural minority. Besides physical appearance factors that also affected the experiences of the participants was the social class, education, religion, ethnic background of the foreign parent and where the participants grew up. Lise who refers to herself as a "visible 'hafu'" was born and raised in Japan by a Japanese mother and an Italian-American father from the USA (Lise and Willer, 2009:3). A limitation of this project was that only two participants were completely born and raised in Japan until reaching university age.

Murphy-Shigematsu's counseling work in multicultural psychology (2000, 2002, 2008) on mixed ethnic and cultural Japanese is the most in-depth study of identity conflicts of any of the writings reviewed. His counseling work deals with Japanese-Americans who grew up and live in the United States, as well as American-Japanese living in Japan, who are the offspring of US military personnel and 'mainstream' Japanese mothers. Murphy-Shigematsu shows how time and place can influence the perception and tolerance of cultural and physical difference. His work with mixed ethnic and cultural Japanese living in Okinawa, in particular, showed how being different can be culturally and politically infused. In his counseling work that focused on the mental health of patients, parental education strategies were seen to be important in the development of a positive self-identity. Murphy-Shigematsu was born in Japan but raised in the USA brings an interesting perspective to his counseling and writing as his father was in the US military and his mother is Japanese. A limitation to these studies is the focus on participants who are of mixed American and Japanese parentage from Okinawa.

Willis (2001, 2008) is the most positive of all the writers about the potential of mixed ethnic and cultural individuals. In his writing about students that attended international schools in Japan, he deals more with a community than with a specific group. He is dealing with a privileged, almost elite group of people, as there are few international schools in Japan, usually located around large city centers and have high tuition fees. As the students of international schools often came from various countries there is a cultural mixing, what Willis calls "creolization, hybridization" (2008:241). Students in effect become "transcultural," not bound in their thinking to any one place, country, culture or group (2001:195). Willis a long-term resident of Japan is married to a 'mainstream' Japanese with two mixed ethnic and cultural sons also has an inside perspective to the issues he writes about as he worked at an international school. A limitation to his studies is that many people that attend international schools come from families with the economic resources to give their children this type of education and are often not in Japan permanently. Also as they attend international schools their exposure and interaction with Japanese people and culture may be limited. Willis also focuses overly on Japan-US relations and his writing often theorizes about the future possibilities for mixed ethnic and cultural students who attend international schools without giving actual examples.

A limitation with almost all of these writings is that parental strategies and non-strategies were inferred by what the participants said about their experiences growing up and the parents were not directly involved in the interviews. Nevertheless, various insights were gained on mixed ethnic and cultural Japanese living in Japan. I will now summarize the findings from these works as they relate to the themes of schooling, language acquisition, cultural transmission, community-social networks, and names.

Schooling Choices

There is a wide range of schooling that mixed ethnic and cultural Japanese in Japan went to. There are those that went to regular Japanese public schools, Japanese private schools, international schools and some went to boarding schools abroad for their secondary school education. Many of the participants started in one type of school and later switched for one reason or the other.

School is seen to affect a child beyond scholastics as it is their first independent exposure to life outside of the home where they can negotiate their place in society. In Japan the public school system with its majority, almost completely 'mainstream' Japanese student body is a like a microcosm of Japanese society in general. In Japanese public schools it is estimated that 98.6% of the students are ethnically 'mainstream' Japanese (Jardine, 2012:2).

Children that attended a public Japanese school often confronted feelings of isolation and marginalization in a majority Japanese context because of their cultural heritage and physical difference (Murphy-Shigemastu, 2002; Lise and Willer, 2009; Kamada, 2010). This would sometimes come in the form of unwanted attention, stares and being asked about their ethnic background. Verbal bullying in the sense of being referred to as *hafu* or even *gaijin* was also common (Murphy-Shigematsu, 2002; Kamata, 2009; Lise and Willer, 2009; Kamada, 2010). Physical bullying by Japanese peers due to their mixed ethnic and cultural heritage was also a problem that came up in a public school context (Murphy-Shigematsu, 2002; Kamata, 2009; Kamada, 2010).

Interestingly, even participants who attended Japanese Saturday schools abroad, in Germany, England and the USA expressed feelings of isolation for being marginalized by Japanese peers and Japanese teaching staff (Lise and Willer, 2009; Kamada, 2010). In one case elementary school-age students were separated by the Japanese teaching staff into two classes of 'mainstream' Japanese and *hafu* Japanese classes (Lise and Willer, 2009). This was in contrast to their feeling of acceptance in the regular public school while abroad where their difference was not an issue and acceptance in the group was a given by the fact of residence in that country and attendance at that school (Lise and Willer, 2009; Kamada, 2010).

For these reasons some parents with children at public schools who experienced or were worried about bullying had a strategy to not attend public schools. Instead, they decided to change to a more liberal-minded and progressive private school that had returnee Japanese students and other mixed cultural students or an international school where ethnic and cultural difference is normal. It is interesting that concern for their children being isolated and possibly bullied were the main reasons for not sending them to a regular public school and the lack of English instruction was second in importance (Murphy-Shigematsu 2008; Kamata 2009; Kamada 2010).

In Japan, the more multicultural, multiethnic and multilingual international school opposed to the monocultural, monoethnic and monolingual public school was generally seen to create an environment that allowed mixed ethnic and cultural Japanese students to focus on studies rather than identity issues (Murphy-Shigematsu 2008; Kamata, 2009). The international school environment is also thought to be conducive to forming an identity that is more multicultural (Willis, 2001, 2008).

A common theme in all the writings is that regular public schools can be a stifling environment for people that do not fit into what 'mainstream' Japanese society has come to expect of 'Japanese' in regards to physical appearance, language, and cultural aptitude. We can see that the Japanese public school with its majority Japanese student body is reflective of Japanese society and its sometimes biased feelings about people perceived to be different. (Murphy-Shigematsu, 2002; Lise and Willer, 2009; Kamada, 2010).

Language Acquisition

The language used at home was shown to be the most important factor in the development of bilingualism (Kamada, 1995, 1997, 2010; Kamata, 2009). When both parents consistently used English in the home the children became bilingual. When both parents were not bilingual and only one parent spoke the minority language, English and the other parent the majority language, Japanese the children became receptive or passive bilinguals understanding most English but usually responding in Japanese. When the children knew that the parent was bilingual and the minority language was not consistently used from an early age the likelihood of the child responding in Japanese was greater and bilingual abilities would be harder to achieve (Kamada, 1995, 1997, 2010).

The amount of contact time between the foreign parent and the child was shown to be a significant factor in becoming bilingual and developing literacy skills in two languages. This was particularly the case when the foreign parent was the stay-home parent made a conscious effort to speak, play and read to the child in the foreign language from the earliest stages of development.

In most cases of international marriage, involving a foreign father and Japanese mother, the mixed ethnic and cultural children were receptive or passive bilinguals but failed to become active bilinguals able to both understand and respond in English. Due to social or financial circumstances, this was seen to be harder for foreign male parents who were the full-time worker (Kamada, 1995, 1997, 2010).

In cases where the foreign mother was the stay home parent but spoke Japanese to the children they naturally did not become bilingual. In order to attain and maintain English speaking and literacy abilities constant reinforcement and total dedication and commitment were seen to be necessary in the overwhelming majority Japanese language environment of Japan (Kamada, 1995, 1997, 2010).

The resources available and used in the home were of importance too. The homes that had the most books, movies and other language resources attained a greater level of success in language acquisition. The more stimuli and English language resources the better and having them in sight and reach of the children were important (Kamada, 1995, 1997, 2010; Kamata, 2009).

Trips overseas or back to the home country were also important and basically the more often the better. An interesting strategy to ensure bilingualism was a trip back to the home country once every five years for a period of one year. In another example more frequent but shorter trips of a month, every year or two also proved successful (Kamada, 1995, 1997, 2010).

Mixed ethnic and cultural children attending international schools or even private schools with an English focused curriculum can be expected to become bilingual and have reading and writing literacy skills in English. But as Kamada (2010) points out, only some mixed ethnic and cultural children attending Japanese public schools become "(nearly) balanced bilingual speakers of two languages" and very few are able to attain "(near) native-like literacy proficiency" in English reading and writing (2010:158). Two of the girls in her study went to Japanese public schools and had reached this level of English language ability. Both had foreign mothers that rigorously applied English speaking, reading and writing skills from the earliest stages of their children's lives.

The educational strategy of second language acquisition comes up often and is mentioned with a sense of regret by the participants who were unable to speak the foreign parent's language and with a sense of personal satisfaction by those that can. It was seen that the ability to speak a second language, possibly even fluently, also gave them greater self-esteem, self-worth and personal satisfaction (Murphy-Shigematsu, 2000, 2002; Lise and Willer, 2009; Kamada, 2010).

Having second language and cultural abilities also gave mixed ethnic and cultural individuals greater cultural capital and status in society, especially in Japan where English is considered to be an important part of the school curriculum (Kamada, 2010). Mixed ethnic and cultural children that did not have the English language abilities or the foreign parents cultural resources or aptitude were considered somehow missing something or deficient by 'mainstream' Japanese in Japan who had this expectation of them (Murphy-Shigematsu, 2002; Lise and Willer, 2009; Kamada, 2010).

Cultural Transmission

Some parents and families made the effort to celebrate popular holidays and festivals from their home country. Christmas and Halloween were mentioned as fun occasions (Kamata, 2009; Kamada, 2010). But the meaning of some holidays such as Thanksgiving and the enjoyment of certain traditional foods was lost on children raised in Japan.

Some common social and cultural norms about raising children in Japan also differed from Western countries. Some of these things were parents sleeping in the same room as children and having a babysitter come over so the parents could enjoy private time together. But the reality was that it was more convenient to sleep in the same room and there is no babysitting system in Japan (Kamata, 2009).

Other culture differences arose when a school disapproved of a mother serving cold cereal for breakfast or making mistakes with the school lunches and not following rules about when to change to long sleeves and short sleeves and gargling after playtime to avoid viruses. The idea of elementary school-aged children walking to school on their own without parental supervision was also mentioned as a cultural difference that was hard for Western parents to comply with when their children were still in elementary school (Kamata, 2009).

Another way of ensuring cultural transmission was extended trips back to the home country or when extended trips were not possible shorter but more frequent trips would aid in cultural learning and understanding (Kamada, 1995, 1997, 2010). The mixed ethnic and cultural participants in these studies showed that whether they grew up in Japan or abroad there was a curiosity to explore their foreign parent's country, the other side of their cultural identity, and when they did they often resolved their self-identity issues. (Murphy-Shigematsu, 2000, 2002, 2008; Lise and Willer, 2009; Kamada, 2010).

The participants who had grown up in Japan and left for periods of time to study abroad or had moved out of Japan expressed feeling more at ease and relaxed in these foreign countries. Being 'different' was not a cause for so many questions about their ethnic and cultural heritage as it was in Japan and in turn they became less self-conscious and introspective (Murphy-Shigematsu, 2002, 2008; Lise and Willer, 2009; Kamada 2010).

Community and Social Networks

The importance of social networks and meeting with other mixed ethnic and cultural families were shown to be important to the parents. This was for their own enjoyment of social activities such as barbecues and to create an occasion for their children to make friends with other mixed ethnic and cultural children and to speak English. In some cases parental support allowed the children to maintain friendships from kindergarten until they were old enough to meet on their own. Some mixed ethnic and cultural children became friends and valued these friendships more than friendships with their 'mainstream' Japanese school friends and were second in importance only to their families. This was especially important as they had no mixed ethnic and cultural role models and as such, they were able to support each other growing up (Kamada, 2010).

Friendships were also made by chance meetings such as at a modeling agency because the ethnic background of the foreign parent was the same. Having siblings with whom they could share their experiences was also seen to be important as was the awareness of others in a similar situation (Lise and Willer, 2009).

It was seen by the experiences of these mixed ethnic and cultural Japanese growing up in Japan that they often felt or were in fact treated as 'outsiders' by peers and Japanese society. As such friendships and groups with others similar to themselves were valuable to them. Some parents seemed to recognize or predict this need for their children but some parents tended to gloss over the mixed ethnic and cultural identity of their children as normal and felt their children simply saw themselves as Japanese but with a foreign parent (Kamada, 2010).

Personal and Family Names

Many of the mixed ethnic and cultural Japanese have a first name, middle name and last name that is a combination of a foreign name and a Japanese name (Lise and Willer, 2009). If this was a conscious strategy or a name change initiated by the participants themselves is unknown but it was seen that a name can be an important piece of one's self-identity, especially when one's name does not match the common stereotypical image of that person's physical characteristics. Murphy-Shigemastu added his mother's Japanese family name later in life and in this way embraced his roots and the full extent of his ethnic and cultural heritage (Murphy-Shigemastu, 2000, 2008).

Conclusion

Most studies up to now have focused on young adults of mixed ethnic and cultural heritage and their search for identity as a minority in Japan. The gaps in these studies have been the focus on adolescents and young adults and their identity issues and not on younger children and parental education strategies. Nevertheless, it has been seen in these studies that parental strategies and their children's identity issues growing up in Japan are not mutually exclusive.

These previous studies have shown that having a physically 'different' look from 'mainstream' Japanese can lead to unwanted attention, teasing, verbal abuse and in the worst cases physical and psychological abuse, especially in regular Japanese public schools. International schools and more progressive private schools seem to not experience these problems to the extent that regular Japanese public schools do (Murphy-Shigemastu 2008; Kamata 2009; Kamada 2010).

Self-identity issues tend to arise in adolescence and find resolution in teenage years or young adulthood. The parents that have applied parental educational strategies that allow their children to gain linguistic and cultural skills not only give their children cultural capital resources for the future but also give them the tools to help with their self-esteem if needed in overcoming self-identity conflicts.

3. HISTORICAL BACKGROUND

In order to understand why visibly mixed ethnic and cultural Japanese would be perceived and treated differently in Japan, it is necessary to see how 'mainstream' Japanese have thought of 'difference' historically. Many ideas and stereotypes from the past still inform Japanese thought today. This is seen in a hierarchy of culture that still exists between the various countries of the world and their social and economic status as compared to Japan; "When foreigners visit Japan, their reception is still determined by the position they occupy in an assumed hierarchy of races and nations" (Taira, 1997:142). In this sense, it can be said that a mixed ethnic and cultural Japanese foreign parent's country, culture, language, and phenotype can affect their social status in Japan.

What it means to be Japanese has had different meanings through the history of Japan. The qualities and we might say the criteria that allow someone to be considered Japanese has also changed depending on the social and political climate of the times (Sellek, 1997; Tsuneyoshi, 2011:5). "In the broadest sense, cultural determinants (religious values, language, patterns of social and economic organization), rather than genetic or physiological markers, have been deployed to signify the existence of an immutable and homogeneous Japanese identity" (Weiner, 1997: xiii).

This 'racialization' or 'othering' of minority groups without reference to phenotype is especially true in the case of the main minority groups of Japan such as the Burakumin, Ainu, Okinawan, Koreans and Chinese who have been treated as "distinct and inferior 'races' without reference to the colour stigmata" (Weiner, 1997: xi). The Nikkeijin is another example of a newer but large minority group in Japan that due to their Japanese ancestry may look 'Japanese' but are linguistically and culturally different and as such treated like an 'outsider'.

As scientific and archeological evidence shows the Japanese are themselves a genetic and cultural mix of various groups of people. The

Jomon and Yayoi people formed the main genetic and cultural foundation of what is commonly thought of as 'mainstream' Japanese today. The Jomon were thought to have originally come to Japan from Southeast Asia and the South Pacific during the Paleolithic period. Then starting in the Neolithic period and continuing in several stages for the next thousand years from about 300 BCE to 700 CE Yayoi immigrants came to Japan from Northeast Asia, particularly Korea (Hall, 1991).

Large-scale miscegenation took place especially on the islands of Honshu, Kyushu, and Shikoku. Ethnic Japanese are thus thought to have attained their present biological and linguistic base between 400 BCE and 1,200 CE (Yoshino, 1992:25; Taira, 1997:144-145). But, since this genetic and cultural mixing took place so long ago, it is rarely considered in discussions about the 'racial purity' and homogeneity of the Japanese people (Weiner, 1997:8; Murphy-Shigemastu, 2008:284).

Looking at three broad periods of time will prove insightful in understanding the main ideas that have influenced Japanese thinking about what it means to be Japanese or 'self' and the treatment of people considered non-Japanese or 'other' during these times. The first ideological period of time takes place during the Tokugawa period from 1600 to 1868. The second period starts with the Meiji period in 1868 and continues until the end of World War II in 1945. The last period encompasses the end of World War II with the occupation of Japan until present times. In particular, China and the West have been "significant others" from which Japan has borrowed models, affirmed and compared themselves (Yoshino, 1992:11).

The Tokugawa Period: Seclusion, Segregation, and Social Stratification

Early contact with European missionaries and traders, particularly Dutch and Portuguese, during the late sixteenth and early seventeenth centuries, brought scientific learning and the importation of firearms. This contact and intermingling with Europeans led to the birth of visibly mixed Japanese children. But in the 1630's Japan officially closed itself off from the world. In many ways, this was a reaction to the fear of Christianity spreading in Japan. As a consequence, "all Europeans except the Dutch were expelled from Japan" (Morris-Suzuki, 1998:81). The Dutch were allowed to remain but from 1641 their movement was restricted to the artificial island of Dejima in the port of Nagasaki (Hall, 1991:188).

The mixed children of Japanese and Dutch were referred to as *Oranda taneko,* children of Dutch seed. The Japanese government "regarded racial mixture" with "horror" but there were "official references to children of Japanese and Dutch parentage during the seventeenth, eighteenth, and early nineteenth centuries" which confirms their continued presence in Japan during this period (Morris-Suzuki, 1998:81).

Beyond their existence, their stories are largely untold. It is assumed that many faced discrimination and various difficulties. However, two positive stories stand out. One is of the son of a Dutch trader and Japanese mother who became a bureaucrat in Nagasaki city. The other the daughter of a German doctor, Franz Phillip Von Siebold, who herself became the first woman to practice medicine in Japan (Morris-Suzuki, 1998).

During the Tokugawa's period of seclusion, the Chinese were also allowed to stay but were also restricted to Nagasaki. But rather than exiled to an island they were confined to *tojin yashiki* or walled ghetto near the port of Nagasaki. "Officially the Japanese ranked the Chinese merchants as 'barbarians' whose status was lower than the Dutch" but "the Chinese trading communities appear to have enjoyed a far higher degree of acceptance than their Dutch counterparts" (Vasishth, 1997:117-118). There were cases of ethnic mixing between Chinese and Japanese and these mixed ethnic and cultural people served an intermediary role in areas of trade and commerce in Nagasaki. The Chinese in Nagasaki were also viewed favorably enough during this time that many poor Japanese without the means to care for their Japanese children gave them up for adoption to the Chinese in the hopes they would have a better education and life (Vasishth, 1997:117-118).

Even before the Tokugawa period China's early influence in Japan was considerable. China was "considered the source of a superior culture and a model of civilized political and social behavior, China was highly regarded by traditional elites in Japan" (Vasishth, 1997:108) Confucianism and the Chinese view of the world as consisting of a "civilized/barbarian dichotomy" influenced Japanese thinking about Japan's place in the world. Civilization was thought of as rings extending out from the center which was China to the periphery in which civilization gradually gave way to the increasing barbarism and unknown of the outer extending rings. Japan adopted this type of thinking of civilization but eventually modified it so that by the end of the Tokugawa period Japan was the center and China and other 'outsiders' were less civilized and barbarian (Vasishth, 1997:113).

Besides the 'barbarian' Dutch and Chinese, the Tokugawa period's caste system also made clear distinctions about the social position and status of Japanese. The four main groups consisted of the samurai, peasant, artisan and merchant classes. The indigenous Japanese outcast group, the Burakumin, fell outside of these four categories. There was a lot of local variation of names and theories of their origin but Tokugawa policies solidified their disadvantaged position in society (Neary, 1997:52-53). As outcasts, they were not considered "fully human" because of the type of work they did which involved working with dead animals as butchers and tanners, handling dead bodies and as executioners and other physically and spiritually 'unclean' work (Neary, 1997:54). The "institutionalized discrimination" of the Tokugawa period led to "social discrimination" in the Meiji period when the classification of the Burakumin as a group was 'officially' abolished. But even today discrimination in marriage, education, and employment is still experienced by the ancestors of these previous outcast groups (Neary, 1997:50).

The Tokugawa period was defined by its seclusion from the rest of the world, the segregation of its foreign population, the social stratification of Japanese society and by the adoption and adaptation of the Chinese civilized/barbarian dichotomy. But as Morris-Suzuki points out there was not "a coherent ideology of race" during this period of time and "the dividing line between "inside" and "outside" often cut across what we would now call "ethnic groups" (1998:82).

The Tokugawa periods rigid caste system and strict isolationist policies proved too inflexible or economically viable to continue indefinitely. Japan was roused from its period of seclusion at the threat of military force by Western foreign powers. In particular "the coming of Perry in 1853 turned out to be an epoch-making event in Japanese history" because Japan signed treaties with America and other European countries and this "signaled the beginning of the end for the Tokugawa Bakufu" (Hane, 2001:70-73). The end of the reign of the samurai marked the beginning of modern Japan.

The Meiji Period to 1945: Colonization, Imperialism, and War

The ensuing ideological transformation of Japan from a feudal to a modern state took place in stages throughout the period starting in 1868 to 1945 and was manipulated by Japan's ruling elite to serve their needs (Gluck, 1985:73). The Emperor became Japan's unifying figurehead and the symbolic link to a pseudo-historical and mythical past where none had existed before (Large, 1997:29; Weiner, 1997:2). This period of time also saw Japan strive to attain cultural and socio-economic parity with Western powers and separate itself ideologically from Asia through colonization and military expansionism (Siddle, 2008:9). The idea of Japanese homogeneity and racial purity also took root during this time (Siddle, 2008:21) and "ideas of 'race' and 'ethnicity' and civilization would be used to create a sense of national solidarity" (Morris- Suzuki, 1998:85-86).

These ideas were supported by Social Darwinist evolutionary theories at the turn of the 20th century (Morris-Suzuki, 1998:85-86). Social Darwinism made it possible for the Japanese "to demonstrate 'scientifically' that some cultures were advanced and civilized while others remained backward and uncivilized" (Weiner, 1997:5). Social Darwinist ideas of 'survival of the fittest' and the ranking of people and societies in a hierarchy ranging from primitive to civilized was used to justify Japanese colonization and military expansionism. The Japanese internal colonization of Hokkaido (1869) and

Okinawa (1879) and the external colonization and annexation of Taiwan (1895) and Korea (1910) and war and military expansionism in China (1894) and Asia (1931-45) were seen as natural and justified in this sense (Weiner, 1997:10-11; Kingston, 2011:40).

These ethnically and culturally distinct people where now legally citizens of the Japanese Empire but with ideas of 'race', 'nation' and 'blood' they were minorities considered and treated as 'outsiders' (Siddle, 1997:24). The Ainu for instance previously thought of and treated as "barbarian" were now posited as a "member of a 'primitive race'" incapable of "progressing to higher levels of civilization" (Siddle, 1997:23). The "attitudes and practices of discrimination learned in relation to Burakumin and Ainu were replicated" when Japan conquered other countries and "when these colonial subjects migrated to Japan" (Taira, 1997:143).

In addition to Social Darwinism Japanese intellectuals during this period debated how to justify Japanese imperialism and colonization of neighboring Asian countries and people who were ostensibly of the same 'race.' Two other popular ideas during this period were "ideas of racial uniqueness" and "ethnic commonalities" all of which "coexisted" at the same time (Morris-Suzuki, 1998:87). The first idea relates to the concept of Japanese homogeneity and the second to Japanese heterogeneity. Japanese heterogeneity, or hybridity theory, in justifying colonization is interesting in that this idea actually emphasized that Japanese people had multiethnic origins and therefore it was logical to colonize neighboring countries and assimilate them into the empire. Assimilation policies by Japanese colonial governments actually encouraged intermarriage between Japanese and colonized subjects. This was especially the case in Korea (Morris-Suzuki, 1998:90-96).

Just as early reverence for China gradually led to Japan ideologically surpassing it the early Meiji fascination and adoption of Western ways similarly led to Japan becoming critical of the West (Hane, 2001:142). The final outcome was war with the allied powers, defeat and the end of Imperial Japan.

The Occupation and Beyond: 'Homogeneous' Japan

The next ideological phase came at the end of World War II with the occupation of Japan, predominantly by the US military. It was at this time that Japan facing questions of war quilt with a morally defeated population and a ruined economy that the Japanese took a more inward exclusive look at what it meant to be Japanese. The Japanese were presented with a new American style "postwar democratic constitution" that "allowed for greater diversity of political ideas but narrowed the idea of ethnic nationality leading to the loss of citizenship for Koreans, Chinese and Taiwanese"

(Morris-Suzuki, 1998:106). These people who were conveniently considered 'Japanese' during military expansion and the building of an empire where now obvious 'outsiders'. As such those that remained in Japan lost many of the rights they had in pre-war years.

The end of the war and the occupation saw a genre of literature called *Nihonjinron* or theories of Japanese uniqueness become popular:

> Many of its major themes can be traced back to the Tokugawa period, although these only really begin to take hold during the period of nation-building following the Meiji Restoration. Defined narrowly, however, Nihonjinron is a post-war product, one shorn of the imperialistic symbolism found in pre-war discussions (Burgess, 2010:2).

This discourse simply put is a discussion of the difference between Japan and the West, especially the USA (Yoshino, 1992:9-11). The discourse of Japanese uniqueness often uses the term *tan'itsu minzoku* to refer to the Japanese people. This term means variously "not only race but ethnic community and nation" thus "racial, ethnic and national categories almost completely overlap in the Japanese perception of themselves" (Yoshino, 1992:25). As such Nihonjinron theories can be used to negate the presence of ethnic minorities and foreigners in Japan and deny them their rights.

In more recent times these assertions of Japanese uniqueness and homogeneity have come from high ranking Japanese officials and even prime ministers. In 1980 the Japanese government in a human rights report to the UN stated that Japan had no minority groups (Weiner, 1997: xiii). In 1986 then Prime Minister Nakasone stated that there were no 'racial minorities' in Japan (Creighton, 1997:224; Siddle, 1997:43). In 2005 and 2007 comments made by high ranking Japanese politicians about Japanese "racial homogeneity" met with no criticism from domestic Japanese media (Burgess, 2007:5).

Visibly Mixed Ethnic and Cultural Japanese in Japan

The occupation and the ensuing relations between US soldiers and Japanese women led to the first large-scale presence of visibly mixed ethnic and cultural Japanese. The history of the terms for mixed ethnic and cultural Japanese is informative of how their perception and place in society has evolved over time.

During the 1940s and '50s the term *ainoko,* meaning "child of two things put together, or a child between two things" was used and held negative connotations of "poverty, illegitimacy, racial impurity, prejudice, and discrimination". *Ainoko* refers to ethnically mixed people but is also a term used for animal breeding. Relationships with US soldiers, the country Japan had just finished fighting, had obvious stigmas attached to them. Furthermore, interethnic marriage between Americans and Japanese was basically unheard of and these children with a visibly different look challenged the 'myth' of Japanese homogeneity (Murphy Shigematsu, 2001; Lise and Willer, 2009). Some Japanese at this time were worried about "half-breed children coming into the world" tainting their 'racial purity' (Kelsky, 2001:74).

Legally these children were not Japanese. The 1899 nationality law was still in use at this time. This system defined citizenship as being based on jus sanguinis meaning genetic and requiring a Japanese bloodline opposed to jus soli which determines citizenship by place of birth irrespective of parent's nationality and citizenship (Sellek, 1997:202; Morris-Suzuki, 2002:165). Furthermore, citizenship was gender biased in that it followed a patriarchal system of inheritance. This designated children with a Japanese father and foreign mother to be Japanese but those with a Japanese mother and foreign father as a foreigner (Murphy-Shigematsu, 2001).

Beyond Japanese discrimination, stigmas and socio-economic barriers during this time, the US government was also responsible for the lack of care and integration of these children. The US government failed to take responsibility for the actions of their soldiers by way of distributing birth control or ensuring that they properly fathered the children. Most importantly Japanese and American marriage was illegal until 1952. These factors led to "massive child abandonment" (Murphy-Shigematsu, 2001:208).

After 1952 marriages between Japanese and Americans became common and many of these children went back to the US with their parents. However, many abandoned orphans remained and lived on the fringes of society. These children whose fathers did not acknowledge paternity became Japanese nationals but were treated as foreigners by society. In Japan and the USA, they were seen as a social problem and an unfortunate but inevitable outcome of the war (Murphy-Shigematsu, 2001).

Ainoko gave way to the word *konketsuji,* which means mixed-blood child. This was a term that also held discriminatory connotations and was also used for other ethnically mixed people such as Korean and Japanese offspring. After the 'official' occupation had ended a large US military still remained and was especially active during the Korean and Vietnam wars. Relations between Japanese women and American soldiers, both in and out of marriage, resulted in the birth of more mixed ethnic and cultural Japanese (Murphy-Shigematsu, 2001).

The continued abandonment of children by military fathers led to the term *konketsuji mondai,* the problem with mixed-bloods, who were seen as social outcasts with identity problems. Due to this negative image "discrimination was experienced by *konketsuji* adults in education, employment, and marriage" throughout Japan (Murphy-Shigematsu 2001:210).

The 1960s saw *konketsuji* becoming popular and some mixed ethnic and cultural Japanese became celebrities. Even with this popularity, "feelings of fascination and admiration for *konketsuji* models and singers was mixed with repulsion of those of mixed ancestry" and as such, they were "objectified and set apart from the majority" (Murphy-Shigematsu, 2001:210). In 2004 a major Japanese newspaper officially acknowledged it would no longer use *konketsuji* as it was perceived to be a derogatory term (Lise and Willer, 2009:9).

The term *hafu* was thought to be first used in the 1930s in Japan but has been widely used from the 1970s onwards. The popularity of this term for mixed ethnic and cultural Japanese was thought to be due to the success of a pop group consisting of four *hafu* Japanese called "Golden Half" in the 1970s (Lise and Willer, 2009:9).

Hafu is derived from the English word half and implies that someone is half Japanese and half foreign. The foreign half can be said to be the side that is emphasized however as the term *quotta,* meaning quarter, is also used to refer to a Japanese person with one foreign grandparent in their ancestry. Though *hafu* sounds odd and even offensive to English speakers it is generally the chosen term used by mixed ethnic and cultural Japanese living in Japan and is not considered a derogatory term. It does perhaps show 'mainstream' Japanese naivety about ethnic and cultural diversity. As *hafu* is originally an English word it is thought to avoid the negative etymological connotations of using a Japanese word like *ainoko* or *konketsuji* (Murphy-Shigematsu, 2001; Lise and Willer, 2009).

The term *hafu* came at a time when the Japanese economy was becoming stronger and the military presence in Japan was less obvious as it was mostly in Okinawa. The parents of *hafus* often came from professions outside of the military. As such a *hafu* in Japanese thinking generally symbolizes an individual who through the foreign parent is bilingual, bicultural and has a stable family life. They may have the economic and cultural capital to go to an international school and travel abroad to visit foreign relatives or even live abroad. This is the idealized image but it is frequently not the reality. Nevertheless, it has created a positive image that other terms from the past have not (Murphy-Shigematsu, 2001).

The foreign half of *hafu* has traditionally implied 'white' with an English speaking parent from a Western country, in Japanese minds usually America. The West is generally typified by America "because of a century and a half of intensive mutual enmeshment at military, political, economic, and cultural levels" (Kelsky, 2001:6). The idealization of the 'white' Westerner as the idealized form physically and culturally can also be seen as a result of this prolonged period of contact, comparison and rivalry starting with the Meiji period and reinforced by the occupation and the popularity of American pop culture (Creighton, 1997:216; Kelsky, 2001; Murphy-Shigematsu, 2001:211).

The 'white' foreign parent is a *gaijin*, literally an outside person, in Japan. *Gaijin* "can be applied to any non-Japanese person" but "it is mostly used for white foreigners who are conceptualized as 'pure gaijin' or 'true gaijin.'" Other groups of people such as "Blacks and non-Japanese Asians" are often referred to as *gaikokujin*, foreign country person or simply as *kokujin*, black person, or *Ajiajin*, Asian person (Creighton, 1997:212). The objectification of foreigners is especially seen in Japanese advertising were they are treated as "misemono, things to look at, and not quite real" (Creighton, 1997: 214).

In 2001 Murphy-Shigematsu wrote that "despite the positive trends, the hafu image is still marred by racial distinctions" because it usually leaves out any group that is not of 'white' and Japanese descent (2001:212). More recent research seems to show some cases of other ethnic and cultural mixes besides 'white' and 'mainstream' Japanese referring to themselves as *hafu*. As Lise and Willer (2009) have pointed out "who belongs and who doesn't belong to the hafu group seems to differ between people regardless of the time and age we live in" which demonstrates "the subjectivity, ambiguity and inconsistency of such labels" (2009:10). The social context and pressure in Japan to conform has up to now meant that those who look like and can 'pass' as Japanese do so to avoid discrimination (Murphy-Shigematsu, 2001:212). With increased positive depictions of different ethnicities and cultures in Japan, people may wish to express their difference more than hide it (Lise and Willer, 2009:9).

Other terms for mixed ethnic and cultural Japanese exist but have not gained popularity. *Kokusaiji,* meaning international child, is perhaps the most politically correct of any of the Japanese terms but it never became popular. It was first used in 1979 and since then mostly in academic writing and formal settings particularly near the advent of the new Japanese nationality law of 1985 (Lise and Willer, 2009:11). The term *daburu,* derived from the English word meaning double came into use in the 1990s mostly by foreign parents with mixed ethnic and cultural children. They wanted to express the wholeness and dual capabilities and possibilities of their children opposed to the negative connotations of the term *hafu* (Kamada, 2010). The term 'Amerasian' is used particularly in Okinawa in a positive sense and the term *Shima hafu,* island half, in a negative sense as it carries connotations of a child abandoned by a military father and brought up alone by a Japanese mother (Noiri, 2011:94).

The popularity of the term *hafu* coincided with increased immigration, both legal and illegal, from the 1970s until present times. Migrant workers came from various countries and increased Japan's cultural and physical diversity (Douglass and Roberts, 2000:7; Ertl, 2010:6; Tsuneyoshi, 2011:131). The "arrival of 'new migrant' workers has presented another serious challenge to the idea Japanese racial and cultural homogeneity" (Sellek, 1998:179). As a result of these ethnically and culturally diversified patterns of immigration and foreigners in Japan, the government has made efforts to create awareness and understanding of multiculturalism in general and as it exists in Japan.

This was originally expressed as *kokusaika* in Japanese, meaning internationalization and is generally thought to be a positive step forward from the discourse of homogeneous Japan (Graburn and Ertl, 2010:6; Kingston, 2011:97). It has also been pointed, however, out that *kokusaika* and similar terms like *ibunka*, different cultures, *kyousei*, co-existence and *tabunka*, multiculturalism are "sophisticated" discourses similar to the Nihonjinron discourse of Japanese homogeneity that by a "process of 'othering' not by exclusion but by inclusion" foreigners are locked "into a particular category of difference" (Burgess, 2004:7-8).

The gendered nature of Japanese citizenship was modified in 1985 so that citizenship would be granted to a child regardless of the gender of the Japanese parent. This allowed all children of mixed ethnic and cultural heritage to be legally Japanese. But Japanese law does not allow for dual citizenship and it requires mixed ethnic and cultural heritage Japanese to choose a country of citizenship by the age of 21. And as there is no racialization of the Japanese census system all traces of a person's ethnic and cultural background are considered inconsequential and are not listed in Japanese records when they become naturalized Japanese citizens.

For this reason, there is no exact figure of how many Japanese of mixed ethnic and cultural heritage exist today in Japan (Okano and Tsuneyoshi, 2011:7). But as can be seen by the high ratio of international marriage, the increasing number of mixed ethnic and cultural babies being born and the continued influx of foreign workers the face of Japan in a physical sense is changing and what it means to be Japanese in a cultural sense is changing.

Conclusion

Minority and foreign groups in Japan have all possessed certain 'differences' from 'mainstream' Japanese in ethnic, cultural, linguistic, social or religious ways. These 'differences' have been used to marginalize minority and foreign groups as 'outsiders' in Japanese society. From the Tokugawa period to more recent times discrimination towards minority groups and foreigners has taken place in Japan. The Tokugawa period saw 'civilized' Japan seclude itself from the 'barbarian' world outside its borders. It also led to the segregation of Chinese and Dutch from 'mainstream' Japanese.

Social stratification within Japanese society led to the indigenous Burakumin becoming an 'outcast' minority group. The Meiji period's nation-building with the emperor as a unifying figurehead gave rise to nationalistic feelings. Social Darwinist, homogeneity and hybrid theories were used to justify internal and external colonization, imperialism and war. The end of the war and the occupation saw the popularity of Nihonjinron literature that focused on Japan's 'unique' ethnic, 'racial', cultural, and linguistic 'homogeneity'.

What is apparent in the past and to an extent the present is a rejection of 'outsiders' and minority groups unless there is a need for their natural or cultural resources or to learn and adopt their perceived positive economic and scientific knowledge or to use them for entertainment or manual labor.

4. METHODOLOGY AND THEORETICAL MODEL

This study used a qualitative interview style approach that focused on parental educational strategies. Eleven multi-ethnic and cultural families with young children living in Osaka Prefecture, Japan where interviewed and data results collected. The qualitative method would allow the participants to explain in their own words their strategies, feelings, and thoughts about various issues about living in Japan. The families as much as possible would be interviewed together to enable me to see the family dynamics and group interaction. In total there were seventy-four questions divided into seven themes. Due to the young age of most of the children, almost all questions were directed to the parents. The seven groupings were (1) Demographic background of the parents. (2) Marriage background of the parents. (3) Orientation of the foreign parent to Japan. (4) Demographic background of the children. (5) Questions for the children. (6) Educational strategies of the parents. (7) Cultural transmission strategies by the parents.

The aim of this study is to examine the educational strategies or non-strategies used by the parents of Japanese children of visibly mixed ethnic and cultural heritage, mainly of pre-school and elementary school age, living in Japan. This study set out to discover what strategies are used to teach the 'foreign' parent's native language, culture and customs to their children. Strategies in regards to types of schooling and travel back to the foreign parent's home country are examined. The reasons why these strategies or non-strategies are employed and the effectiveness in teaching their children about their bilingual and bicultural heritage are explored.

The types of strategies or non-strategies used would provide perspective on family priorities but also on possible pressure to conform to social norms in Japan today. As such, this study wished to explore the reasons why these strategies or non-strategies are used with these questions in mind: Are they used to avoid identity conflicts, bullying or other forms of discrimination? Are these younger children perceived and treated differently by extended family, classmates and by 'mainstream' Japanese? Are they treated and do they feel like 'outsiders' or as Japanese or a mixture of both and is this something that is dynamic and good or confusing? Is growing up *hafu* in Japan 'normal' in this day and age or do factors like the nationality, physical characteristics and gender of the foreign parent change how the child is perceived by 'mainstream' Japanese society? Do socio-economic and cultural hierarchies consciously or unconsciously still exist in Japan today?

The families interviewed consisted of a 'white' foreign parent married with a 'mainstream' Japanese parent. This would provide a more focused study of a specific type of 'visible' minority group. This study would also highlight a smaller percentage of the types of international marriages taking place in Japan. And as the stereotypical image of a *hafu* is generally a person with a 'white' English speaking parent and a 'mainstream' Japanese parent these families would provide an interesting look into the present day aspects of the *hafu* phenomena. A further aspect of this study is that these children all attend regular public schools and live in a smaller semi-rural city interspersed among the majority Japanese population.

There was one interview session with each family that lasted about two hours. The interviews were conducted with families that live in my town or in nearby neighboring towns. My personal contacts consisted of eight families. Four further participants were contacted by using the snowballing method in which by word of mouth I was introduced to friends of friends who I had never met before or had only met in passing and did not have their contact details. One Japanese woman, in particular, the wife of a friend who had agreed to do the interview, was very helpful in trying to recruit people to help with the research project. She had many contacts through an international marriage group she participates in and helped me get in touch with three participant families. Eight of the twelve families live in my city of residence, Kawachinagano City, three live in neighboring towns and one family lives in Osaka City but the father works in my town.

Kawachinagano City, Osaka Prefecture

Kawachinagano City in the southeastern part of Osaka Prefecture where most of these families live provides an interesting look into the changing ethno-cultural landscape of Japan today. Kawachinagano feels a lot more like a town than a city and is in many ways different culturally and economically from an international city like Tokyo. Kawachinagano is a 35 minute express train ride to Nankai Nanba station, the southern hub of Osaka city, but there are no major shopping malls, movie theaters or Starbucks there. It can really be considered semi-rural as rice fields and rivers are scattered throughout its borders with many mountains nearby.

There are also no major manufacturing industries like Toyota or Sony though it is somewhat famous for its toothpick, *sudare* bamboo blinds, and sake production. It also holds some small historical notoriety as a stopover on the way to and as a part of the *Koyadou*, a route Buddhist pilgrims took on their way to the Koya mountain monasteries. Today it is a collection of suburbs referred to in Japan as a 'bed town'.

The population of Kawachinagano City is 114,157 people of which only 545 are registered foreigners accounting for only about 0.5% of the population. This is less than the almost 2% in Japan but similar in that the majority of registered foreigners are Asians. There is one public kindergarten and ten private kindergartens and various private nursery schools in Kawachinagano City. There are thirteen public elementary schools, seven public, and one private junior high school and there are two public and two private high schools in Kawachinagano City.

Table 1: Registered Foreigners by Country (Kawachinagano City)

Total	South Korea	China	Brazil	PHL	USA	DPRK	India	Canada	UK	other
545	252	94	49	36	19	10	8	7	6	64

Source: http://www.city.kawachinagano.lg.jp

Theoretical Model

My approach to this study is influenced by the multicultural Japan discourse and is theoretically similar to the more recent re-evaluations of it. The multicultural discourse refutes the homogeneous Japan discourse and its main argument that the Japanese are a homogeneous people, *tan'itsu minzoku* who constitute a racially unified nation, *tan'itsu minzoku kokka* (Burgess, 2004:5). More than mere literary musings these notions of homogeneity have been expressed on multiple occasions by various Japanese politicians (Burgess 2010:11) and are widely accepted as truth by the general 'mainstream' Japanese population (Murphy-Shigematsu, 2001:216). The multicultural Japan discourse in its efforts to refute the 'myth' of homogeneous Japan has been criticized for over-emphasizing the 'differences' of minorities and foreign groups which ironically gives credence to the idea of the 'uniqueness' and 'homogeneity' of Japanese society (Burgess, 2004, 2007, 2010; Murphy-Shigematsu, 2008; Okano and Tsuneyoshi, 2011). More recent discourses of Japan as multicultural move away from this static view of minorities and foreigners as separate groups to focus on "interactions among individuals of diverse cultural backgrounds and inter-group multicultural interactions" and the "strategies adopted" by these people who are categorized as 'other' in Japanese society (Okano and Tsuneyoshi, 2011:2).

This study agrees that Japan is a multicultural society that involves the interactions of people of various ethnicities and cultural backgrounds but acknowledges that it forms a small part of the whole which is still made up of mostly 'majority' Japanese. This study looks at marriage between non-Asian foreigners with 'mainstream' Japanese and their educational strategies for their children. This study shares the view that multicultural change is taking place and is best understood by looking at "the dynamics of particular localities" where diverse groups often in small numbers have naturally come together and interact with one another and with 'mainstream' Japanese (Graburn and Ertl, 2010:5). As such this study operates from the belief that multiculturalism is happening at the local grassroots level and would argue that change is happening in even more random and unpredictable ways than the idea of "diversity points" would suggest where 'foreigners' and minorities are still seen generally grouped together by area of residence (Tsuneyoshi, 2011:150).

Other research emphasizes the positive aspects of mixed ethnicity in Japan and for those with bilingual and bicultural proficiency highlights their capacity for greater cross-cultural understanding (Willis, 2001, 2008; Murphy-Shigemastu 2008). This study agrees that this could be the case but would argue that to attain a high level of bilingualism and biculturalism parental strategies and the socio-economic factors of the family are of key importance. Furthermore, and more importantly, this study puts forth the idea that even without complete bilingual and bicultural proficiency these visibly mixed ethnic and cultural Japanese due to their visible difference will positively and naturally increase ethnic and cultural awareness and create a constructive discourse about ethnicity and multiculturalism in Japan.

Limitations of the Study

This study was limited by a number of factors. The participants formed a rather small study group and the foreign parents were of a somewhat similar ethnic background. The participants also generally lived in or near the same small city in Japan. The contact time with the families as a group was also minimal. A further limitation was that as I knew some of the participants personally and was in a similar family and lifestyle situation I needed to be aware of possible personal subjective bias in my interviews and interpretations of answers. Some of the limitations, however, could also be considered a positive as a small focused study group of similar type families, that have randomly come to live in the same general area of Japan, could provide a valuable piece of the puzzle of change taking place in Japan today.

Ethics Review

As this study involved young children an ethics review was submitted to a university ethics committee. Following university procedures, a completed ethics application form and a participant information letter were written explaining the details of the study in which the confidentiality and voluntary role of the participants were explained. Following the approval of these documents, possible candidates were contacted and a letter of consent was signed by the participants.

5. DATA RESULTS

The data from the interviews are presented in themes. The first theme looks at the general background of the families and the foreign parent's orientation to Japan and feelings about Japan. The second theme looks at parental educational strategies for their children. Educational strategies will be separated into language at home, home strategies, choice of schooling and future schooling plans. The third theme is strategies for cultural transmission. The fourth theme will look at the participant's experiences and reactions to being perceived as different and posited as an 'outsider'.

General Background of Participants

Of the eleven families that participated in this study, there were nine foreign fathers and two foreign mothers and all were 'white' Westerners (see Table 2). Compared to recent Japanese statistics on immigration and international marriage the participants of this study constitute a smaller percentage of the majority which consists mainly of Asian females. In this sense, these families can be considered a minority among minorities within Japan. As these children are Japanese they in many ways constitute the most obvious visibly different looking type of Japanese people in its history.

Of the nine foreign fathers, four met their Japanese wives outside of Japan in their home countries or in one case another Western English speaking country while traveling abroad. Two of these four were married before coming to Japan. All other families were married in Japan and all the children were born and raised in Japan except for one child who was born and lived in the USA until she was 2 years old.

That four of the eleven families initially met abroad is interesting in that it constitutes a large percentage of this study group. It is also directly linked to the mass emigration, travel, and study abroad by Japanese women during the 1980s through to present times. Japanese women in particular, in far greater numbers than Japanese men, left Japan during these periods for travel, study abroad programs and work (Kelsky, 2001:2).

Table 2: Background of Participant Families

Name	Age	Children / Age	Nationality	Occupation	Years Japan	Years Married
1.Ben(M)	40	2(12/8)	American	Teacher	14	9 divorced
2.Ivan(M)	40	2(3/2)	Croatian	Teacher	5	5
Kanami(F)	34		Japanese	Housewife		
3.Mark(M)	31	2(4/1)	Canadian	Teacher	7	6
Tomomi(F)	34		Japanese	Office worker		
4.Pierre(M)	46	2(8/5)	Canadian	Teacher	11	9
Kanon(F)	41		Japanese	P/T worker		
5.Emily(F)	42	4 (18/16/ 14/4)	American	P/T worker	26	18
Toshi(M)	58		Japanese	H.S. Teacher		
6.Steve(M)	39	3(8/6/3)	American	Teacher	8	9
Mayumi(F)	34		Japanese	Housewife		
7.Tom(M)	40	3(6/3/1)	British	Teacher	8	7
Ayaka(F)	43		Japanese	Housewife		
8.Linda(F)	38	2(7/5)	Canadian	P/T worker	14	9
Kazu(M)	43		Japanese	Skilled laborer		
9.Will(M)	46	3(8/3/2)	Australian	Teacher	10	8
Wakako(F)	40		Japanese	Housewife		
10.John(M)	44	2(9/6)	Australian	Teacher	16	11
Satomi(F)	40		Japanese	J.H.S. teacher		
11.Ron(M)	54	1(4)	Australian	Teacher	7	5
Hiyori(F)	39		Japanese	Housewife		

The other participants came to Japan for various reasons and since they could earn money teaching English while experiencing Japan made the decision easier. One foreign parent came to Japan on the Japan Exchange and Teaching Program (JET). Two other foreign parents came to teach English at what was one of Japan's biggest foreign language schools (NOVA) and were recruited for the job in their home country. Two others came to join friends from their home country who were already working in Japan. One came to teach English by himself and another came with her father, who had come to Japan for work, while she was still in high school.

Looking at the families involved in this study we can see the average age of the participants is 40 years old and that the average age of the children is about 6 1/2 years old. There are 2.36 children per family which is higher than the Japanese average of 1.43 and similar to the international marriage fertility rate in Japan of 2.9 children per family (Graburn and Ertl, 2010:21). The foreign parent has lived in Japan for an average of about 12 years. The couples on average have been married for 8 years and dated for about 3 years before getting married. In all eleven cases, the foreign in-laws were accepting of a Japanese marriage partner. However, in three cases the Japanese in-laws were opposed to marriage with a foreigner:

(Laughter) In the beginning, my mother don't want marriage with Ron because from another country. She don't want mix another countries blood, but now very happy (Hiyori).

The father did not accept the wedding, the marriage. When we first told him we were dating he told to us to quit dating. When we asked him to accept our marriage he refused... flat out kicked us out of the house, told me to go back to America and her to stay in Japan... For him it wasn't so much us as it was the children, he felt they would have a confused identity, which he was very much against... but once we came back to Japan married... and especially after she was born (oldest daughter) he has been completely warm and accepting (Steve).

They (Japanese in-laws) weren't happy and they basically disinherited him (Japanese husband). So I have only met his mother once and never met his father (Emily).

For the other participant families, there was basically no problem with acceptance by the Japanese in-laws but in two cases the Japanese wife was already several months pregnant with the first child. Even from this small sample of eleven families it can be seen that there is still some lingering stigmas and apprehension attached to international marriage and mixed ethnic and cultural children in Japan.

Initially, no one had a long-term plan, at least beyond two years, for staying in Japan. Though some of the participants possess skills in other fields their main asset is their natural ability to speak English. This linguistic capital they possess which is a requirement in Japanese education, a necessary skill for many Japanese workers and a pastime for many language enthusiasts enables them to make a living in Japan. They also have the natural ability to pass these skills and forms of social, cultural and linguistic capital onto their children. All the foreign male participants work as full-time English teachers and the foreign female participants teach English part-time. The availability of English teaching jobs and particularly the demand for native speakers of English is still high in Japan.

The reasons, however, for coming to Japan were not expressly to find work and make money. People came for "fun" and "to hang out" for "curiosity" and "adventure" to "pay off school loans" to "meet friends" or be with their family, girlfriends or wives. And of course to experience Japanese culture but they did not need Japan strictly in an economic or political sense. They made a choice of their own free will to come to Japan. They are not here as illegal immigrant workers etching out a living in the obscurity of a factory and they did not come as foreign brides to marry Japanese men in the increasingly depopulated Japanese countryside in the hopes of a better life and standard of living (Graburn, Ertl, and Tierney, 2010). The main reason for staying in Japan is that, in the absence of a long-term concrete plan, life took its 'natural' course of getting married and starting a family. With a steady income, a decent standard of living and the relative safety of Japanese society most families felt that Japan provided a satisfactory environment for them and their family.

The foreign husbands work as full-time English teachers and are basically earning a middle-class income. This is one of the reasons that most of the Japanese mothers are the stay-home parent or work part-time but are not the full-time worker. The monthly income is roughly the equivalent of a middle-class Japanese worker but the foreign parent, like many foreign teachers in Japan, does not receive the same monetary benefits as their Japanese counterparts in regards to the usual twice-yearly bonuses, lump sum retirement annuity or company/school retirement pension plans. More importantly, most foreign teachers in Japan do not have the same job security that their Japanese counterparts do who are tenured or as public school teachers are civil servants with essentially guaranteed employment.

Foreign teachers are almost always contracted workers employed on a yearly and sometimes three-year basis with the chance to renew at the end of the contract period. The contracts, however, might not be renewed and this is a cause of stress and worry during renewal periods. Foreign teacher's livelihoods are thus left to the whims of their employer, Japanese demographics and prevailing economic conditions.

In regards to how long the participants plan to stay in Japan answers varied. In fact, since the time of the interviews, three families of the eleven have already moved back to their home countries. A fourth family also moved back for about a year but as the father did not find a sufficiently stable job the family came back to Japan. The remaining families had no set plans but foresee living in Japan at least until their children reach university age. An indication of many of these families overall satisfaction with life in Japan is that five of the eleven families have bought homes in their areas. Whether living in Japan was better for the foreign parent personally rather than living in their own country answers varied:

It is better for me to live in Japan because it makes me more entrepreneurial... it challenges me more and I have more ambition to develop teaching techniques... It does inspire me more than working back home (Mark).

Depends, as far as lifestyle goes no but... career wise, work wise it's easier here in Japan. There are good and bad about both. I miss the lifestyle back home, the social thing, just being able to have a chat with another foreigner. I can't stand the summers (heat and humidity) (Tom).

For me personally no, if it was just me, oh definitely! (Australia would be better) (Ron).

I don't know because I came here when I finished University. So I just started working here. In Canada, I just had part-time jobs. So if I would have stayed at that time I probably would have got a job and done a career. But I didn't do that, I came here, so now I am teaching English and I'm making good money and it's good. It might have been different if I had some sort of career in Canada, then I could compare the two. But, now I am thinking of going back to Canada and I am excited about that too. So it was good while I was here (Linda).

As far as living in Japan as a family most participants felt Japan has both positive and negatives aspects. In particular, Japan's low crime rate, fewer social problems and the ability to make a good living teaching English were considered very positive aspects of life in Japan. The feeling that the education system, especially from junior high school to university level, is very rigid in that it focuses on entrance exams and rote memorization opposed to creative thinking was generally considered a negative aspect of life in Japan for their children. The focus on study opposed to free time and group-oriented activities at the expense of individuality was also a negative:

It has its good sides and bad sides I think. The good sides are I would say like it is socially stable and there is not so big crime rate or social problems… education system is convenient, basically, it's not so expensive as it is in the States… from that point yes. From another point, I wouldn't want them to grow up here… There is big pressure put on kids to constantly study, study, study, to be part of society, to do group activities that maybe they don't want to do it but they are pushed to do it, that kind of things I don't like… (In Japan) they learn to live to work rather than work to live (Ivan).

Financially Japan is better and safety wise Japan is better but my views on education don't coincide with the Japanese views on education. So educationally and individuality wise I think the States would be better and I would be happier to have my kids raised over there because I think they would have more freedom to be who they are and there wouldn't be this huge stress on them about exams and getting into the schools (Emily).

I feel comfortable with both of them (Japan and Canada) but as far as education I feel that elementary school is very good in Japan but secondary school is a little better in Canada because it's less studying and more thinking. Its more research and they learn to be more independent. But at the same time, there is more drug problems and violence problems in Canada. Especially in big cities that I don't feel there is in Japan. But then Japan there's other problems. Sociability and lack of opportunity to be with their friends, to be a little bit more free, to go out and be a little bit more independent. There is really good points and bad points (Pierre).

OK right, there's different things. OK, now that we're going to move back (to Canada) I am looking forward to some things but have bad feelings about other things. Like I don't think I will let my kids go out to play by themselves in Canada. So I feel like it's safer here. And I feel like people don't stick their nose in your business as much here (Japan). There's not someone telling me to do this and that so much as in Canada (Linda).

Kids learn a lot more in Canada because they have free time, unstructured time, to do much more whereas in Japan there's so much structure and rigor that your constantly being kept to a time schedule where you have to be doing this at this time and this at this time. Canada your done school at 3:30 and you have summers where you can do all these different things and experience more (Mark).

For kids, living in Canada is better. Kids can speak English in Canada but not Japan. I want (kids) to be native speakers of English (Tomomi).

Language at Home

As many of the children in this study are very young and their language abilities are still developing it is difficult for me to assess their linguistic abilities. It is also beyond the scope of this study which sought to look at parental educational strategies to examine detailed linguistic aptitude. However, from my perspective as a native speaker of English and as an English teacher the abilities of the children to comprehend what was being said in English but who were not able to respond in English, receptive and passive bilinguals, and those children with the ability to comprehend and respond in the second language, active bilinguals, specific cases stood out to me. In some cases, the children were only able to communicate in Japanese.

It was seen that the ability to understand and respond in English had a direct relationship to the language used at home from the earliest stages on. The two cases in this research project where the foreign parent was the mother stand out for the English speaking ability of the children. In both cases, the mother was the stay-home parent and the language spoken with the children was English. Both mother's Japanese ability is of a basic level but more importantly, they had a strategy to use only English with their children. Both foreign mothers had a policy of speaking only English with their children and even when the children tried to speak Japanese to them they insisted on using English and would only answer the children if they spoke English.

"When the kids were born we created an English only home environment. We only spoke English. So their mother tongue actually is English" (Emily). When I asked Emily what she would do if her children spoke Japanese to her she said, "I just don't listen to them, basically." The other foreign mother Linda, said something very similar about not using Japanese with her children, "If they speak Japanese I don't answer them. I say I don't know what you are talking about". These foreign mothers who had spent all day every day with their children from the time they were born could use this strategy of demanding English from their children because they knew they understood and could speak English.

Some foreign fathers also had this strategy of using only English with their children. In some cases, this was due to the fact of not being able to speak Japanese very well but it was also a conscious strategy on their part. The effort of some foreign father's was obvious in that the children understood English quite well but the ability to respond to questions in English and speak English was limited. This was in sharp contrast to the language abilities of the children with foreign mothers who were the stay-home parent opposed to the fathers in this study who were the full-time worker.

For the foreign fathers involved in this study, it would perhaps be unreasonable and impractical to demand only English from their children as the mothers in this study did because their children grew up in Japan raised by their Japanese speaking mothers. In the nine cases involving a Japanese mother, all spoke only Japanese with their children.

Some couples had made plans to speak only English with the children or create an English only household but these plans proved too difficult to maintain for the Japanese parent. Occasionally English was used by the Japanese parent when helping the child who didn't know how to say something in English to the foreign parent, particularly the father, or sometimes when using simple phrases in English but otherwise communication between the Japanese parent and child was in Japanese.

Many foreign fathers that could speak Japanese used a mixture of Japanese and English with their children. This would often take the form saying something in English followed by the Japanese meaning of what they had just said or switching to Japanese when the topic of conversation became more complex. In some cases almost all Japanese was used by the foreign father:

> I am not here that often. I work long hours every day… they see me for a little bit in the morning before I go to work and in the evening for a little bit before bed and so… I would love to speak English with them but you know it's like that little bit of time we have together would end up becoming an English lesson. They spend all day long with Mom living their life in Japanese and then Dad comes home suddenly speaking English… it just facilitates things to speak Japanese and make things go a little bit smoother (Steve).

Communication between husband and wife for all eleven families generally included a mixture of both Japanese and English. Between siblings the language of communication was Japanese. The children with foreign mothers spoke either Japanese or English to each other depending on the situation.

Speaking only English and not Japanese is important and needs to be a conscious strategy especially in Japan because when children get older and leave the home and enter the all Japanese world outside using English with the foreign parent and siblings becomes a challenge. The two cases were the mother was a foreigner and the language in the home and between family members was English gradually met with resistance and their stories are telling of the difficulties of maintaining an English only environment in Japan:

Just the past few months, I don't know this year, Ryoma is going to grade one, when they (siblings) talk about only Japanese things, they speak Japanese (to each other)… So as their world is getting bigger they're speaking more Japanese to each other. Like since he's been in grade one, she's in kindergarten, the Japanese things they do together (has increased), but they're still 70% English (to each other)… When we all lived together at home, like before they went to school, we only spoke English (Linda).

As they got older they stopped trying to talk to me in Japanese. They all hit a point around second grade (elementary) to junior high where they would try the Japanese on me but once they got to about the end of junior high they quit trying (Emily). Tim: You should probably write a book on how to do that. Emily: (laughs) Yeah, just don't learn Japanese!

Educational Strategies at Home

Beyond speaking English to their children many parents tried to use English with their children in various ways and using different types of media. Some parents who taught children's English lessons from their home would have their children join the classes. Some parents would make a weekly English language class for their children to have a chance to practice English with them. Some parents would read bedtime stories to their children in English. Many parents took advantage of the availability of the various types of video conferencing software to talk with foreign relatives once a week or a few times in a month. Many families watch movies and TV series in English. Some families also had Japanese cable TV that offers many English language programs like Kids Station, Cartoon Network and the Disney Channel. Computers and tablets were also used by many parents to play educational games and watch English language content programs or uploaded material on YouTube. One foreign parent said that playing multi-player video games with his son provided a great opportunity to speak English because they would talk about the game and the necessary strategy as they played together as a team.

The frequency in which these English sessions took place varied from a from a few minutes to an hour a day to once a week set English language lesson or in some cases only watching a movie in English a few times a year. Most of the parents mentioned how their children happily watched cartoons and movies in English when they were young but as they got older, generally from about 4 years old, they wanted to watch the programs in Japanese and not English. The Japanese language had taken hold and in order to avoid crying, tears and a fight most foreign parent's allowed their children to watch TV in Japanese.

Choice of Schooling

All families made a choice to send their children to their local Japanese public elementary school. This choice was partly due to practical and financial considerations. The nearest international schools to Kawachinagano City are a long commute away and tuition fees are expensive. But when I asked hypothetically what if there was a reasonably priced international school located nearby almost all of the families said that as far as elementary education was concerned they would still probably choose a regular local Japanese public school. The fact all families expressed their overall satisfaction with Japanese elementary education was based in large part on their children learning Japanese language and culture. Many families, however, felt that the Japanese elementary education system would be better if it was more progressive in the sense of fostering more creative thinking and individuality. Most families felt that learning English would naturally take place in the home and were not overly concerned with the level and frequency of English instruction at elementary school:

We sent her to the normal school and quite frankly that was the best thing because she got to know all the kids in the neighborhood, she plays kick-baseball and she's amongst all her friends. That's the best way to learn Japanese culture… Japanese primary school, I think is superlative in the world. It's a lot better than Australia. They really nurture children here (John).

If we could afford it and it was closer sure, probably, but to be honest though it's a close choice. I mean Jin getting complete exposure to Japanese culture here naturally and shifting along equally with the other kids with their *kanji* and spoken language and so on. Hopefully, he will be right up there with the rest of the kids as far as that is concerned. And of course, have the opportunity at home to speak English (Will).

Not the international school, but maybe a private Japanese school, if I could afford it, but even then the problem I have with that is a lot of the kids and people that go there are a very closed society, like they have this attitude that we are better than the general population and I don't want my children to pick up that attitude… I'm living in Japan so I feel should take advantage of them learning Japanese and I can teach them English at home so that's why I sent them to the public (school) (Emily).

Not really. I'm satisfied with Japanese schools. It's actually a really good system here (Ben).

Going to a regular Japanese school has a lot of merits too, right, because he can learn a lot of the Japanese culture that I can't teach him properly, he can learn a lot more about the history which I want him to, especially *kanji*, I'd love him to learn *kanji* and know it right… I figure he will speak English anyways, no matter what (Mark).

Future School Plans

Almost all the families mentioned their feelings that the Japanese public education system from junior high school would not be their first choice or the best option for their children. Many families expressed that from junior high school and high school a private Japanese school or an international school would better:

For me, its Ema's schooling. I don't want her going to Japanese junior high schools or high schools (Ron).

I wouldn't want to send Kana to Japanese public school for junior high school or high school (Satomi).

Chugakkou (junior high) it would be fun for him to have a more international crowd around him then it would be interesting. *Shogakkou* (elementary school) they shouldn't be bothered with this. They're still kids so they just have fun. But *chuggako* it's an occasion to experience more people, more culture and they understand more what's going on around them… maybe an international school would be better (Pierre).

Basically, I would not educate them in Japan… My original thing was when she (oldest daughter) started junior high school when she finished sixth grade, was to move back to the States. At that point, they would have a solid understanding of Japanese and then they could continue their education in English but it didn't work out like that… if we had the money and the means we would go back to the states" (Emily).

Some families expressed the hope that their children would be able to study abroad in their home country or another English speaking country for a year of junior or senior high school. Most parents felt that education abroad for university studies, in particular, would be better than Japan:

I want to send them to high school in Australia but we haven't decided... (Will) wants them to go university in Australia. I think Australia education is much more, higher than Japanese university (Wakako).

I want him (oldest son) to go to university but not in Japan... I would like him to go maybe in *chugakkou* (junior high) or *koukou* (senior high) and spend a year in Canada come back to Japan and finish his high school and then go to university in Canada or elsewhere... I frankly think that university is better in Canada than it is in Japan (Pierre).

I hope one day, I really hope that they can each get the chance to go for a year or more of high school but it doesn't look like it's going to work out. But I hope that one of them or a few of them would choose to study or go to college in the states... I think it would really benefit them (Emily).

Three children from two different families have attended regular public schools in the USA for a period of one year. Two of the children are siblings who returned to the USA with the Japanese mother for one year when they were in kindergarten and the first grade of elementary school. Another girl went to the USA for one year of high school and stayed with her mother's family.

These three participants all had a good to an excellent level of English listening comprehension. The girl that went back for a year of high school spoke English fluently. This participant's foreign mother had also always spoken English to her children at home. The girl that went back for a year of elementary school in the first grade was also the child that was born and raised in the USA until she was two years old and she spoke English as a near-perfect bilingual. Her father is the foreign parent and though divorced he has joint custody and spends a few days of the week with his children speaking in both English and Japanese to them.

The girl, now in the sixth grade, likes English movies and music and this is another factor in her maintaining a high level of listening and speaking ability. Her younger brother who also went back to the USA for a year, but was born and raised in Japan, was not as proficient in speaking English. He often code switched between Japanese and English or would substitute Japanese words for English while speaking in grammatically English patterned sentences.

Almost all parents expect that their children will be bilingual regardless of where they attend school or end up living in the future. Most parents felt that knowing English would be an asset in the future as it has basically become an 'international' language and that culturally they would like their children to be able to communicate with them and extended family members in English. One family, however, was quite frank about not needing English and said that speaking English is not the "key to happiness". But even these parents that did not speak English in the home felt that when their children grew up if they wanted to learn English they could always go back to the foreign parent's home country for a year and learn English at that time. Some parents also mentioned that if they were to return to their home countries they would make an effort to maintain the Japanese language and traditions inside the home to preserve that side of their children's cultural background.

Cultural Transmission

All foreign parents came from Western and for the most part, English speaking countries that had their belief systems rooted in Judeo-Christian traditions; though most foreign parents did not strictly adhere to any particular religion. Most of these families were quite secular in their beliefs and lifestyles and almost all families had a cultural hybrid approach to special occasions and holidays in which they celebrated both Japanese and foreign traditions.

These Japanese and foreign holidays were generally celebrated with a focus on commemorating a special occasion and as an opportunity for family time rather than for overtly religious and cultural reasons. For instance, Christmas, though popular in Japan but more as a date night among young couples was celebrated in a Western way with a Christmas tree and gifts for all family members and with some gifts from Santa too. Japanese holidays like the Buddhist holiday of *Obon* in August in which families visit the grave site of relatives who have passed away to give their respects was followed. The Japanese Shinto tradition of *Hatusmode*, visiting a shrine in the new years to pray for health and prosperity and eating traditional New Year's food *Osechi*, was observed by most families. In fact, most Japanese holidays and customs were followed.

Some parents, particularly those from Canada and the USA, lamented that certain traditions and holidays were hard to do in Japan; a traditional Thanksgiving dinner was almost impossible to replicate in Japan because it was hard to find a turkey in Japan and an oven big enough to cook it in. This and the fact that the meaning of Thanksgiving in Japan was unknown meant that this holiday was generally passed on by most families.

Halloween is another occasion in Japan, like Christmas, that has gained popularity but is not celebrated in quite the same way as North America. Usually, Japanese children that go to English language schools might have a costume party with some games and snacks. The main difference is that children do not go trick-or-treating in Japan. Some foreign parents would make a costume party at their house with Halloween decorations and have trick-or-treating at their door. One family organized a trick-or-treating event on their street and asked the Japanese neighbors to participate. Another family would have a few of their children's friends over for a party and instead of doing trick-or-treating outside would go to every room of the house instead.

Many families traveled back to their home countries. The frequency of the visits varied but the average was once every three years for a period of three to four weeks. The frequency of visits did not seem to have a direct relationship with English speaking ability. Taking the two foreign mothers as examples one went back to her home country to visit family and friends once and often twice a year for three to four week periods but the other had only been back to her home country once with her children as a family yet the children from both of these families have very good English speaking abilities.

But, as far as fostering cultural awareness in the children that they are from two different cultures, these trips did seem to create this understanding. These trips also helped the children realize the need for English to communicate with relatives and people living outside of Japan. Many of the children answered that they liked the foreign parent's country and this seemed to have a lot to do with the fact that when they had been back it was for vacation and was a fun time and a good memory. In this sense trips back created a positive image of their foreign parent's country and helped the children understand they have relatives in that country and are from a mixed cultural background but live in Japan.

Of the eleven families, three have already moved back to the foreign parent's home country and one other family went back only to return about a year later because the father could not find satisfactory employment. The general feeling from these families was that they basically like Japan but their home country would be a better place overall for their children. There was a feeling that it was time to move on and in particular to a country with a more multicultural environment and lifestyle where being a bit different didn't carry as much weight. This was something that Japan was not providing for these families:

The reason why we are moving back (to Australia) is not because we hate Japan or we don't like Japan or that we think Australia is better it's because we want these two (children) to be bilingual, bicultural, while they're young (John).

Feelings on Being Treated as an 'Outsider'

Many of the children interviewed quite simply looked different than a 'mainstream' Japanese child. Gauging what 'different' means is of course subjective but the spectrum of difference ranges from very light skinned with light colored, rarely but sometimes, almost blond hair to darker skinned with darker features more resembling an 'Asian' looking person. Naturally the Japanese parent and the 'white' foreign parent's darker or lighter features contribute to the look of the child. One interesting feature to note is that visibly mixed ethnic Japanese children basically never have green or blue eyes and even the blonder colored hair turns to a light brown or brown color as they get older. Sometimes even among siblings one will have a more 'Asian' or 'Western' appearance from the other. As such in the eyes of 'mainstream' Japanese some children have an obvious *hafu* 'look' and may even be considered foreigners by appearance alone but others may not and only occasionally be considered or asked if they are *hafu*.

One amusing exchange between two siblings in this study took place when the older sister mentioned how their Japanese mother said the younger brother looked "a little (bit) Mexican" and when asked what the older sister looked like the boy said she had an "America *kao* (face)." Another funny story was told by a Japanese father who recalled a one day when he was out with his 'foreign' looking daughter who was throwing a tantrum and crying loudly that he became worried people would think he was a kidnapper and not her father because they looked so different.

Because of or in spite of this 'rarity' due to their obvious visible difference there seem to be no major problems with the children of this study being accepted by their community and peers. This acceptance needs to be qualified in that it depends on their familiarity within the community and peers. The first reaction these children often receive by Japanese when outside of their usual surroundings is that they are *hafu* and even *gaijin*. The latter is often the case for those children with fairer skin and lighter colored or curly hair.

A Japanese mother and her son from this study were out grocery shopping one day when they were met with shouts of *"gaijin, gaijin!"* from a group of older youths. Another family mentioned a story about when their daughter was on a school outing and riding a train with her classmates some children from another school called her *"gaijin"* in an insulting way. The homeroom teacher called the parents to relate the details of the story because it seemed the daughter was upset by the incident.

A teenager from this study said if people ask if she is *hafu* she says "yes" and if they ask if she is a *gaijin* she also says "yes" because she can't be bothered going into the details of her ethnic background with strangers. A father mentioned how it becomes annoying when Japanese say or even blurt out, *"kawaii!"* a compliment meaning cute when they see his daughter because even though it is a compliment it makes for too much constant attention focusing on her physical appearance. Here we see two examples of even when there are no negative feelings attached to the questioning of ethnic difference it can become tiring to be the focus of curiosity:

Because, always when I go somewhere, like when I first went to school (children) were like *'gaijin, gaijin'* (Ryoma 7 years old).

One thing I care about is that they stare at me. People stare at me. It's OK if they ask (where I'm from), but I don't like that they just stare at me... I don't think it's bad, but I don't like that they stare for a long time... I just don't look at them, but if they stare at me I think that something is on my face because they look at my face because I'm a little bit different. So, I always ask my mom if something is on my face and she says, 'no' so I'm like OK, it's my face (Minami 12 years old).

Yeah, I had my first experience with that at the park, yeah, they (children) were playing with her (daughter Ema) and getting along real well. And the two little girls were playing with her and they went back to their grandfather and said in Japanese that they had been playing with that *'gaikokujin'* (foreign country person). Ema wasn't listening. And I just thought, wow that's the first time I've heard them say that and I wondered how she would react when she does hear that. She didn't hear it and I was glad she didn't hear it. And then I thought, we have to go back to Australia. I don't want her to have to put up with that (Ron).

Being different and particularly visibly different in Japan can still be a cause for surprise, curiosity, fascination, and even contempt but the signs are that things are more positive than even a few years ago. Many of the parents expressed that these changing attitudes towards mixed ethnic and cultural Japanese are sometimes positive and sometimes annoying in that mixed ethnic and cultural people are stereotyped in a certain way as being different:

It's cute because its half. It's a good meaning in Japan. When we (Japanese) say he looks half its compliment. They (Japanese) admire, envy. But it depends on the nationality because they are half-Western, Caucasian, but if they were half Black I don't know, it's maybe different story because impression is different (Wakako).

50/50 means half. It's not negative. It means both. Now it's positive (Kanon).

Sometimes Ema comes to my group lessons and they still treat her as a novelty. They don't treat her like she's a Japanese kid. It's like 'Oh, she speaks perfect Japanese!' She is Japanese. She has only lived in Japan. And I say it to them. I say look, she doesn't speak English. It's not a big deal but they go 'Oh, it's amazing, oh, Osaka *ben* (dialect)!' But she lives here that's her language. And I think that's because she looks Caucasian (Ron).

There is this expectation that they can speak English. Sometimes we will run into people in town, 'there so cute, can they speak Japanese?' People just see them and make that instant assumption that *hafu* children speak English. But, you know, you have people like Becky and Wenz on TV now it's really starting to change people's perception which is good. Here in the neighborhood where there are other kids (*hafu*) that have already paved the way for them... neighborhood kids are used to mixed nationality kids (Steve).

At this date in time it's easy for them, 20 years ago it wouldn't have been this way... The face of Japan is changing. Foreigners of all sorts are taking advantage of living in Japan... There's a lot more mixed kids. There's a lot more Japanese marrying outside races... There is a very positive attitude here in Japan now that is accepting of that whereas in the past it wasn't... I am exceedingly happy that they have a good life in Japan... When I was back in the military here I knew people that were raised here *hafu*, the stories they told were horrendous... *hafus* had it pretty rough... they don't have it rough here at all now, they are almost idolized (like TV celebrities)... right now I'm happy that they are having a great life here now and have choices... but if they were bullied all the time and they couldn't reach their potential... but now they are totally clear of all that... Japan with the media and movies has come full circle and they have a good life here and they have a good grip on the future... so I expect them to chase their dreams (Ben).

Still, many parents expressed fears and anxiety about discrimination towards their children as they got older or at some time in their life in Japan. The parents expressed that discrimination could happen anywhere in the world but that it was more likely to happen in Japan and they hoped that their children would be mentally and physically strong enough to stand up to these possible situations:

> Yes, a little bit because different color, different face, *'gaijin, gaijin'* (Hiyori).

> I feel as they get older they will be looked at more as the opposite that they are very lucky, fortunate and gifted. It might be more of a plus as they get older. But they will definitely have issues. There will always be someone that gets in their face because someone doesn't like Americans. Hopefully, it doesn't happen too often (Mark).

> He has pale skin and they know his father is a foreigner so he might get teased for this. But I hope I can help him reason his identity (Pierre).

> In England, it's a lot more multicultural than it is here. Even now it's not very multicultural here (Japan). I still think it's kind of a bit racist here. In Japan, it's not really fine to be different. If you're not part of the group and you don't fit in you are weird or I don't know. I don't like that kind of attitude really. So being *hafu* is different and you don't fit in... I am more worried about it happening (discrimination) in Japan than in England. In junior high school especially or even elementary school, I'm not sure. In Japan, the school she goes to she'll probably be the only one (hafu) (Tom).

> Yes, I think so because of their name and they look different. I think Japanese people generally they don't like someone to be different especially when they are kids (Aya).

When I asked the parent's their feeling about the word *gaijin* all the Japanese spouses said that it did not have a bad meaning. The foreign spouses, on the other hand, had a variety of answers ranging from dislike to ambivalence but none of them actually like being called a *gaijin:*

> I would say 80% of the time when it is used by Japanese it has no negative meaning. It can't possibly be used today as it was used in the historical sense of Perry and the Dutch (Ben).

> I feel Japanese have a different prejudice against other Asian countries. Sometimes a little bit scared of Africans, they feel scared, insecure. The white race they feel both envious, distrust and respect at the same time... The *gaijin* word is certainly not as bad as the 'n-word' or 'paki' (Pierre).

It doesn't have a bad meaning (Tomomi).

It depends on who says it… It bothers me. I don't like it much (Mark).

I definitely agree that the way it is used can determine whether it's a racial slur or not. To be honest, when people are trying to be polite they tend to use *gaikokujin* (Steve).

Generally, I don't like it. I think it separates people I totally get that most people don't mean it as a slight (Ron).

The question of what nationality the children are seemed to pique the most interest from the foreign parents. There was usually a slight silence before their child answered the question and the foreign parent's anticipation of what their child might say was palpable in that instant. Many parents had said beforehand that they had told their children that they were of both countries and that they usually answered as such. But when I asked the children what nationality they were almost all said that they were Japanese. Some said both or that they felt like they were both but this was only a few children. Some were too young to really have an understanding of nationality or what country they were from, basically the children three years of age and under, but they understood that one parent spoke Japanese and one spoke English or that one was from Japan and one was from another country where foreign grandparents and relatives live.

When I asked the children if they were *hafu* all the children old enough to answer said yes because that is how Japanese have always referred to them. All of the children have had experiences of being called or asked if they are *hafu* or *gaijin* in Japan.

Conclusion

The parents that took part in this study have been a combination of a Japanese parent and a 'white' Western English speaking parent making the children a visible minority in Japan. Most foreign parents try to teach English to their children by speaking with them in English. Other strategies include watching TV, DVD movies and YouTube programs in English. Other strategies are reading books and playing games with their children. Many families also used software such as SKYPE to talk with relatives and English educational websites available through the internet.

The children's English ability is dependent on the contact time with the foreign parent. A major factor in the children's English language ability was whether the stay-home parent was the native English speaker. In the two cases, where the stay-home parent was the native English speaker who made a point of speaking only English to their children from birth onwards, the children became active-bilingual speakers of English and Japanese. In these two cases the children developed a very natural almost 'mother tongue' level of English. In the other cases where the native English speaking father was a full-time worker but made an effort to speak English to the children, the level of English developed at a slower rate. In these cases, the children showed an understanding of what was being said in English and occasionally responded in very simple English but usually in Japanese. Parents that did not speak English to their children or use any English type of activities to any great extent and basically spoke Japanese with their children the English level was very low.

Parents are generally satisfied with Japanese schooling at the elementary level but express dissatisfaction or worry about schooling from the junior and senior high levels. The fees and availability of alternative schooling like international schools or bilingual schools or high-level private schools that may have more progressive curriculums with more English or multicultural content limit the parent's present and future options. All the children are attending public schools and the younger children are attending regular private Japanese nursery schools or kindergartens.

Almost all families celebrate both Japanese and Western traditions, for example celebrating Christmas but also visiting a shrine in the New Year. For some parents, the opportunity for their children to meet or have other mixed Japanese children in the same town or school is comforting to them. The idea that their children would have peers in a similar situation that could help them get along better and ease the possibility of feeling like an 'outsider' was reassuring. One family's children did part-time modeling for a Japanese fashion agency and the Japanese mother felt that her children were more relaxed and had more fun when speaking English with the other children at the modeling agency.

It seems that the parents that have made efforts to participate in Japanese society and make Japanese friends as well as having foreign friends or groups that they can join helps with their personal sense of satisfaction about life in Japan and with their feeling that Japan is a good place to raise children. This seemed to be more important for the mothers than the husbands.

From an early age, the children are aware that they are somewhat different. This realization comes from the presence of the foreign parent and from visiting the foreign country and meeting foreign relatives but also from their Japanese surroundings where peers and strangers will ask them if they are *hafu* or even *gaijin*. This seems, however, to have little effect on their self-identity which is that they are Japanese with a foreign parent. The older children in this study show that the idea of being different seems to increase with age, generally from upper grades of elementary school through junior high school. With the support of family members and friends resolution to any identity conflicts seemed to be resolved.

The recent widespread celebrity status of other half-Japanese in the media seems to help their self-identity. Most parents, however, worry or feel that their children will inevitably face some sort of discrimination or even bullying at some time in their life because Japan still has very few visible minorities and is not as multicultural as many Western countries. Some of the children have already experienced being 'othered' by 'mainstream' Japanese.

Three of the eleven families interviewed have returned to the foreign parent's home country. Another family left Japan only to return about a year later because they could not find satisfactory employment in their home country. These families expressed the feeling that being different in Japan could lead to possible discrimination but they mentioned this could also happen in their home countries. More than anything the idea of having their children growing up bilingual in a more relaxed multicultural society was the main factor in deciding to return to their home country. The desire to be near family members was also mentioned as a reason for leaving Japan.

6. DISCUSSION

As a 'white' foreigner *gaijin*, from Canada living in Osaka for many years, I have experienced an interesting mixture of fascination, admiration, envy, distrust, and even dislike from 'mainstream' Japanese to varying degrees on occasion and what has been referred to as "petty discrimination" in Japan by Japanese (Kingston 2011:96). Two personal incidents of this pettiness were not being allowed to open a bank account at a certain Japanese bank and not being allowed into a bar because *gaijins* were not allowed, *"gaijin dame,"* meaning literally foreigners no good but basically meaning no foreigners allowed. On this particular bar occasion, it was only a Japanese friend and me. The two of us were a rather innocuous pair.

On two other occasions when alone and entering retail stores I was not greeted with the usual respectful, *irrashaimase* or welcome but instead with a very cool, *"nani?"* literally what or what to do you want? I did not buy anything from these stores but they probably would have begrudgingly sold me something. These are not life changing events because there were other banks, stores, and bars that wanted my business but they were frustrating and are indicative of the somewhat precarious reception a visible minority might receive in Japan. These incidents also stand out because the pettiness was not from some random individual on the street but from service industry organizations.

A famous legal case about discrimination against foreigners is from a long-term resident of Japan, Debito Arudou an American 'white' Westerner, who became a naturalized Japan citizen. Arudou is a voice for minority rights in Japan and one incident that stoked his fire was being denied entry into a public bathhouse in Hokkaido, Japan because he was a visible minority. The bathhouse even posted a sign in three languages; Japanese, English, and Russian which read: "JAPANESE ONLY". The excuse the staff gave for denying entry to foreigners was that they had problems with Russian sailors not following bathhouse rules. That day

Arudou was with a group of Japanese but there was also a Chinese woman with them and when they pointed out to the staff that she was Chinese they realized their mistake and said that she would be denied entry too. When Arudou, who has two mixed ethnic and cultural Japanese daughters, asked if they would be allowed entry the answer was that only one of the two daughters would be allowed in; the 'Japanese' looking daughter but the more 'foreign' looking daughter would be denied entry (Arudou, 2004). The discrimination involved in this incident is troubling because it was based on arbitrarily perceived physical differences in which 'Japanese' looking foreigners could enter but Japanese nationals that did not fit the stereotypical 'mainstream' Japanese 'look' were denied.

From random Japanese, there is a wide spectrum of reactions you might receive as a foreigner. Japanese for the most part are kind and helpful. Once when I was still new to Japan and unable to withdraw money from a Japanese bank machine with my foreign bank card, I must have looked flustered enough that an older lady nearby actually came up and offered me some money, which I politely refused. Sometimes in Japan, as a 'white' foreigner, you are treated as an "honored guest" (Lie 2001:172). A neutral ambivalent feeling is the most common or mild curiosity to the occasional English language enthusiast who will try their English out on you. More often than not you get stared at for longer than is comfortable or someone in their surprise at seeing a foreigner will say *"gaijin"*. Most of the time there is no malicious meaning but occasionally due to the context of the situation and tone of voice a negative intent can be perceived. Sometimes you know that as a visible minority you are the butt of someone's joke.

Years ago, I went golfing with a Japanese friend and we were the only two warming up hitting balls on the practice range when a golf cart with four Japanese passed by and yelled, *"gaijin!"* and broke into uproarious laughter as they looked our way. My friend seemed embarrassed and I was annoyed by it. When you are a visible minority in Japan this type of reaction and behavior; rudeness, immaturity, petty discrimination, call it what you will, can happen. When you mention these types of incidents to Japanese the usual response is that it is meaningless, harmless excitement at seeing or meeting a foreigner. Granted sometimes this is the case but sometimes it is just rude. In the last few years, with more and more tourists visiting Japan, the novelty of seeing a 'real-life' foreigner seems to be waning and these types of incidents are less frequent.

In Japan, I am a foreigner, and I came to Japan as an adult and chose to live here and raise my family here but no one feels good about being reminded they are an immigrant or a foreigner. People want to called by their name and if they are a foreigner by their country of birth. Japanese do not like being categorized as Asian or East Asian but as Japanese. The children participants of this study are Japanese and not foreigners so if they are referred to as *gaijin* it takes on a deeper negative meaning that could affect self-confidence and lead to self-identity issues.

Finding a Topic

As someone living in Japan with a multicultural family and due to my experiences as a visible minority the idea to do research on children of mixed ethnic and cultural heritage living in Japan was a natural one. The idea was given further impetus while reading about ethnic minorities in Japan. The books and articles raised my awareness of the various minority groups in Japan. But as someone married to a Japanese wife and with two children of mixed ethnic and cultural heritage I was left with the feeling a chapter was missing. My circle of friends and co-workers in similar situations to myself, not to mention the ubiquitous presence of 'celebrity' *hafus* on TV, in various media, and in professional sports made me feel this was the case and not only a topic of personal interest to me but of social relevance to present-day Japan.

My initial goal was to interview as many multicultural families with mixed ethnic and cultural children as possible. I also hoped I would be able to meet and interview families in which the foreign parents came from a wide variety of countries in which language, culture, and physical look differed. This would have provided an interesting broad comparison of experiences of people from different cultures and how they are perceived and treated in Japan.

To this end I contacted two acquaintances who live and work in my town and volunteer at a type of international friendship association; this NGO group referred to as *kokusai kouryu* or international exchange, helps foreigners living in the city and creates opportunities for cultural exchanges with Japanese. The two women, one from Nepal and the other from the Philippines, were eager to help and willing to do the interviews themselves but as one is married to a Nepali and the other married to a Japanese but without children, I was unable to include them.

They asked members from their group to participate and the initial response seemed promising but in the end, I failed to get any volunteers from this group. I was told that many of the foreign women, mostly Chinese and Filipino married to Japanese, were busy with work and taking care of their children and that they did not speak English very well. I mentioned that the interviews could be done in Japanese but they said they were busy and if they could just have a questionnaire to fill out they would participate. I was somewhat left with the feeling that they did not want to meet in person and wondered if they did not want to bring unwanted attention onto themselves and their families as the children have grown up in Japan and could basically 'pass' as Japanese physically and culturally.

The idea of being able to 'pass' as Japanese and the idea of visibly mixed ethnic and cultural Japanese being considered *hafu* was made apparent in my second interview. This interview was with a friend who is a third generation Japanese-American married with a Japanese wife and has two children who were born and raised in Japan. My friend is culturally American but after many years in Japan, his cultural and linguistic proficiency is very high. In a legal sense, he is a foreigner but visibly to a stranger on the street he is Japanese. His children were in the fifth and sixth grades at the local public elementary school. Their 'Japanese-ness' has never or rarely been questioned. Japanese peers and strangers have never stopped to stare or ask if they were *hafu* or *gaijin*. Only once did the older boy come home while in the upper grades of elementary school and ask his father if he was *hafu* because his father was American. During the course of the interview, it became apparent that his children are basically growing up 'Japanese' and do not really fit the 'popular' definition of the term *hafu*. In some ways they are culturally *hafu* due to their American father but they have lived their whole life in Japan with only occasional trips back to the USA, they speak very little English, use a Japanese family name and in the sense of 'bloodline' they are completely 'Japanese' as their ancestors in the USA only married with other Japanese. For this reason, this family's data was not used in this study.

In the end, it seemed to me that there were gaps in the research about the early childhood and family lives of visibly mixed ethnic and cultural Japanese. And as childhood is the foundation for adulthood I decided to study younger aged children and their parent's educational strategies. The study found its target and narrowed its focus to multicultural families consisting of 'mainstream' Japanese and 'white' Western parents raising their visibly mixed ethnic and cultural Japanese children in Japan. The Japanese people who are referred to as *hafu* in Japan.

A Rather Ordinary City

The setting of Kawachinagano City where this study took place and where most of these families live shows that Japan, even outside of big city centers with large foreign populations and international schools, can be an adequate place for mixed ethnic and cultural families to live and raise children. The small percentage of foreigners and even smaller percentage of visibly different foreigners in Japan becomes an even smaller percentage of the whole in a place like Kawachinagano City.

At the schools the children who participated in this study attend they are often the only visibly mixed ethnic and cultural child. The three elementary schools I teach at in Kawachinagano City there is a student body of 684, 565 and 162 students at each of the three schools respectively. At the first school, there are only two visibly mixed ethnic and cultural Japanese children. One child has an Iranian father and a Japanese mother and the other child has a Peruvian father and a Japanese mother. These two children due to the foreign parent's physical characteristics are in my opinion only slightly visibly biracial. At the second school, there is only one student and his mother is Jamaican and father is Japanese. This student 'looks' more Jamaican than Japanese; he is well liked by his classmates but to some extent, he is treated as a visiting guest and not just another Japanese classmate. At the third, school there are none.

At some schools there are no visibly mixed ethnic and cultural Japanese children or the foreign parent is an Asian foreigner and the children may have or use a Japanese family name and as they 'look' Japanese they are not considered *hafu*. It may not even be known that they have a foreign parent unless the children make a point of telling others they do and as such they could 'pass' as a 'majority' Japanese.

As mentioned Kawachinagano City is a smaller city, almost semi-rural with no major industry, hotels, tourism, English language school chains, international trade or business to speak of. The percentage of foreigners living there is relatively low so the question of why this place would be considered a decent place to raise a multicultural family, opposed to a cosmopolitan city like Tokyo or more foreign populated areas of Kobe for instance and why would multicultural families be accepted there comes to mind. The answer perhaps is due to a few factors.

Kawachinagano City has for over twenty years tried to be progressive in regards to offering English lessons at the public elementary and junior high school level. One of the thirteen elementary schools and one of the seven junior high schools were at one time Japanese Ministry of Education English language pilot schools for a few years. The pilot elementary school had English lessons several times a week for all six grade levels. The other elementary schools in the city also had regular English lessons, but less frequently and usually from the middle grades of elementary and upwards, once every other week or about twice a month for an average of 18 classes a year. These classes were team-taught by a foreign English teacher and the Japanese homeroom teacher. As English is still not a mandatory subject at the elementary level in Japan this paltry amount of English and contact with a foreign teacher can be considered progressive by Japanese public school standards. This was especially the case 20 years ago. It could be said that this minor exposure to English and a foreign teacher at the schools has helped foster a better attitude towards foreigners and multicultural families in the city.

There is also the international friendship group in the city which tries to help foreigners by offering Japanese classes or assistance with other aspects of living in Japan. This group tries to promote international awareness and cultural understanding by showcasing the foreign volunteer's culture at various city events and festivals with food, crafts, and traditional clothing booths. These type of events can be criticized for promoting ideas of Japanese uniqueness because the foreign culture is shown in a stereotypical way and in contrast to Japan's 'unique' culture. But there is still real human interaction taking place and this could help broaden Japanese opinion of foreigners and be another reason for the city's acceptance of multicultural families.

And lastly four Japanese wives from this study, three from Kawachinagano City, met their husbands while abroad and ended up returning there with them and starting a family. This shows the desire to learn English and speaks of an open mind in regards to experiencing a foreign culture by the women themselves and most likely by their parents as the daughters were single at the time of their study abroad. This also shows that some Japanese families in the city have economic capital and are willing to use it to increase their linguistic and cultural capital by joining study abroad programs.

These are some of the reasons that Kawachinagano City has provided a safe and normal environment to live. But these reasons alone are not exclusive to Kawachinagano City, which on the whole is a fairly unremarkable place, and these various elements exist in different cities throughout Japan. Perhaps this rather ordinary city speaks of Japan's greater acceptance of ethnic and cultural difference in general.

It could also be indicative of the randomness of discrimination and reception foreigners and mixed cultural families might receive. Just as I was refused at one bank when I first came to Japan but the next bank in the same town was happy to have me as a customer. One family in this study mentioned how in the previous city where they lived, also in the Kansai region of Japan, that they were actually told that mixed families were looked down upon in that city and not exactly welcome there. The individual with whom they spoke may have been merely expressing his personal opinion and cast his feelings on the whole town but the family mentioned it as being an uncomfortable interaction.

Language and Culture

During the interviews with these families, it was seen that they felt that Japan was an adequate country to raise a family in regards to social, economic, educational and political aspects of life. All the families shared the hope that their children would embrace and be proud of their mixed ethnic and cultural backgrounds. The families generally had a relaxed attitude about their children growing up in Japan and most expressed the simple wish that their children would be happy in life. But there was also a desire and expectation that the children would be bilingual and that they might possibly study at university abroad. At the moment most of these children's English ability would make this a very difficult endeavor for them to achieve. It has been seen that mixed ethnic and cultural Japanese children attending regular Japanese public schools rarely become fully bilingual, bicultural and biliterate (Kamada, 2010). For most of the children in this study who are very much immersed in Japanese language and culture, it would be very difficult for them to do so. It was seen that "parental laxness" in regards to bilingualism often led to the failure of the children becoming bilingual and led to feelings of "regret" on the parent's part for not being more proactive (Kamada, 1997:53).

In regards to English language ability the children with the two English speaking mothers and the child who was born in the USA and stayed in the USA during the first grade of elementary school had very good speaking abilities. Surprisingly even other parents whose children's English ability was very low felt that if their children wanted to become bilingual and bicultural they could always just go back to the foreign parent's country for a year and stay with relatives. But as seen by one family in this study even though one child was able to study for a year abroad the option might not be available for other siblings in the future because of changing family dynamics and economic considerations. Many families are also teaching their children English at home but as the children get older and busier in their academic and personal lives this may become an educational strategy that will become difficult to maintain.

Culturally these children are Japanese but enjoy a somewhat hybrid cultural experience due to their foreign parent and occasional trips back to the home country. But the longer these children live in Japan immersed in an all Japanese environment the less likely their abilities and perhaps desire to successfully leave Japan become. As one parent said about his life in Japan and that of other foreigners, "some of us who stay over here actually end up with nothing to go back to, even though we'd like to" (Ben). This is due to economic reasons and because family members move, grow older or pass away. Over time as these possible avenues back to the foreign parent's home country vanish for the parent, they also vanish for the children.

Quite simply becoming completely bilingual, bicultural and biliterate is very difficult in Japan. This realization is a major factor that led to three families leaving for their home countries and a fourth who left only to come back to Japan for economic reasons. For these families, bilingual and bicultural hopes and expectations were not being achieved in Japan. The families that moved back said that they would try and maintain a Japanese language and cultural home environment in their home country. Though it may seem more acceptable to be different in a more multicultural country it may still be hard to raise children to be bilingual and bicultural.

Furthermore, the children may not be willing to do so and the effort and result will not be different from trying to do the same in Japan.

Discrimination and Bullying

Overall parents felt positive about their mixed ethnic and cultural children growing up in Japan but expressed some fears that they could experience discrimination while living in Japan at some time. It has been seen in other studies that mixed ethnic and cultural Japanese who are bilingual and bicultural achieve greater social and cultural capital which in turn creates greater self-confidence and a more positive self-image than mixed ethnic and cultural Japanese who did not have these abilities. A positive self-image which came from the knowledge of the foreign parent's language and culture allowed the mixed ethnic and cultural Japanese to overcome bullying by their Japanese peers and discrimination in Japanese society in general.

Even in case studies where bullying was not a problem it was seen in previous literature that mixed ethnic and cultural Japanese developed an interest in their other ethnic, cultural and linguistic side as they grew older. Individuals that had experiences with the foreign culture and abilities in the foreign language where seen to be more confident and content individuals. Beyond the obvious advantages of being bilingual, bicultural and biliterate it was seen that 'mainstream' Japanese have this expectation of visibly mixed ethnic and cultural Japanese and when these expectations are not met it somehow lowers their status in Japanese society (Murphy-Shigematsu, 2000, 2002, 2008; Lise and Willer, 2009; Kamada, 2011; Noiri, 2011).

The choices parents make will be seen to be important in their children's development of a positive self-identity. As a visible minority in Japan complete and unquestioned membership in society by 'mainstream' Japanese at all times and in all places and contexts will not always be the reality of these mixed ethnic and cultural children. In Japan today outward appearance as much as Japanese linguistic and cultural proficiency still dictate and inform popular opinion about a person's place in society.

As the young children of this study have already been posited in a similar way as 'outsider' *hafu* or 'foreigner' *gaijin* in Japanese society it would be a good idea for the parents to make increased efforts to have their children tap into and embrace the foreign side of their linguistic and cultural heritage. As one of the older girls in this study expressed her 'difference' and English ability became a source of positive social and linguistic capital as she grew older and was something her 'mainstream' Japanese peers wanted but did not have; "They (Japanese peers) become interested in us because they realize how important English is in junior high school. They can't speak English and we can" (Jenna).

The children participants in this study have luckily not been met with severe discrimination or bullying but they have been teased and at times made to feel different because of the way they look. During the interviews, the children old enough to express themselves in Japanese or English did mention some situations where their mixed identity was stressful for them. It was usually recalling an episode among their peers at school or when outside of the home at a shopping mall for instance or just the general reaction they get when going to a new place and meeting new people for the first time. Sometimes concrete incidents came to mind easily but at other times it was like they were expressing a general feeling about their physical difference and how the attention can be stressful.

Parents should be conscious that their children are possibly internalizing some stressful incidents and are either too shy or unable to express their true feelings about being different. As one parent is Japanese and the other parent is a foreigner they cannot know exactly what their biracial children are going through growing up in Japan. As the oldest girl of this study said in regards to the challenges they might face, when talking about one of the celebrity *hafus* that are now prominent in the media, "I don't know her life story but if she was born and raised in Japan she must have had the same type of problems we did so we have something in common and it makes us want to cheer for her" (Jenna).

The Nail That Sticks Out

The popular Japanese proverb about the nail that sticks out gets hammered down is particularly apt in conveying Japanese social and cultural requirements and expectations in regards to proper use of language, behavior, social etiquette and physical appearance in both a sense of fashion and grooming. Just being a 'regular' Japanese person in Japan with all its unwritten rules can be demanding. This proverb about social conformity and group over individual mentality may take on an even more ominous meaning and carry a greater burden for visibly mixed ethnic and cultural Japanese that look different and may sometimes act or think differently from the 'majority' Japanese population.

Some of the children participants in this study have experienced stares, teasing, and occasional discriminatory remarks. Other biracial Japanese have sometimes faced more serious episodes of discrimination. Ariana Miyamoto, Miss Universe Japan, experienced discrimination as a child growing up in Nagasaki, Japan for being half African-American in appearance. In elementary school, some of her classmates did not want to hold her hand during a school outing because they didn't want her blackness to rub off on them. Another school incident was during a gym class, some students refused to swim with her because they thought the water would be dirtied by her dark skin. She has had garbage thrown at her and been called the 'n-word'. She said she decided to run for Miss Universe Japan to be a voice for biracial Japanese people. The suicide of one her biracial Japanese friends due to self-identity issues especially influenced her to be more socially active (Saberi, 2015; CBS, 2015). Suicides in Japan for being of mixed race have been reported on occasion (Mainichi, 2010). The obvious positive aspect of the story is the fact that later in life she was voted Miss Universe Japan. This points to the changing perceptions and greater acceptance of visible minority Japanese. But unfortunately the acceptance was not unanimous and the praise was tempered by debates and even criticism on social media about her not being Japanese enough to represent Japan (Serio, 2015).

These types of incidents help to understand why someone would be content to 'pass' as Japanese if they could. This is, of course, only possible if the person resembles the 'majority' Japanese population enough to do so. A high school friend of my wife and her naturalized Japanese husband, whose parents are Korean, is this type of Japanese. This man had never talked to me about his Korean roots even though I had spent some time with him at various outings. I somehow felt he didn't want to talk about it and though I was curious I never asked. And since he was born and raised in Japan and had adopted a Japanese surname no one really knew of his Korean background. Of course, if family records were checked at city hall it would be shown that his ancestors came from Korea. His Japanese wife's parents knew of his ancestry and had vehemently opposed the marriage for this reason, even though he was what one would consider a stand-up citizen and had a respectable job as a firefighter.

This couple came over to my house for a family Halloween party and one of the other Japanese family's children wore traditional Korean female dresses, *chima chogori,* as their costume. When my friend casually mentioned the choice of costume being traditional Korean dress, the Japanese mother, with a nervous smile, was very quick to point out that she was Japanese and that she chose the costumes because she thought they were cute. She certainly didn't want to be considered Korean and an 'outsider'. My friend just nodded politely but did not bother to mention his Korean roots or carry on the conversation any further.

Sometimes someone looks Japanese but the name is different and this can lead to discrimination. My Japanese wife uses my family name and this on at least one occasion has led to her being harassed at work by a customer. She was working part-time at a Japanese confectionery shop in the food court of a large Japanese department store. As all staff wear name cards her foreign name which was written in katakana, the Japanese script used for foreign words, was visible for customers to see. This one time a Japanese man in his fifties took issue with her foreign name and harassed her verbally by repeating her surname several times aloud and saying in a loud voice, "what are you a foreigner, are you a *gaijin?*" making a fool of himself and being a nuisance for her and her workplace. This man was alone and it ended there but had he been inebriated or in a group it could have made for a stressful and even dangerous situation.

These are a few sample stories of incidents that could basically take place on any given day in one form or another in Japan. Generally, it's these flashpoints of individual discriminatory or racist feelings that arise in Japan which are usually more annoying than outright racist or life threatening and are often just ignorant and immature. Racism and discrimination is not institutionalized like it was during the Tokugawa period with is caste system but right-wing 'racist' nationalist groups do exist and will gather in the form of demonstrations in which they will verbally harass and threaten minority groups; especially Koreans living in Japan but other minority groups have been targeted (McNeill, et al., 2009, Saberi, 2015). On the whole, Japan is a safe country but for minorities, there is a sense that discriminatory feelings might be lurking beneath a veneer of civility and can bubble up to the surface at unexpected times. This can inevitably leave minorities in a defensive and vulnerable position in Japanese society.

A Tale of Two Seals

The lack of multicultural awareness and sensitivity sometimes seen in Japan is encapsulated in two rather odd stories involving seals. The first incident revolved around a seal that kept showing up in a Yokohama river inlet in 2003 and caught public and media attention. The seal was considered cute and was affectionately named "Tama-*chan*" after the river where it was first seen. "*Chan*" is a term of affection usually used for children. The seal basically became a local icon and caused a media frenzy with crowds flocking to watch and photograph the bearded seal. The story was on national TV and even goods of the mammal were sold.

Had "Tama-*chan*" been returned to his natural habitat the story would have had a nice ending but controversy arose when "Tama-*chan*" was awarded an honorary residency certificate or *juminhyo*. This raised the ire of Japanese minority groups such as ethnic Koreans and Chinese, who have lived in Japan for two or three generations and had their Japanese citizenship stripped from them after World War II, and other long-term permanent residents who are not eligible to have a residency certificate even though they pay residents tax. By law, they must always carry an alien registration card on their person.

A residency certificate gives a person more independence as it allows for greater access to financial institutions such as when applying for loans or renting an apartment and simplifies dealing with governmental bureaucratic issues. The resident certificate also acts as a registry of the members of all Japanese families but since ethnic groups and foreign nationals are barred by law from receiving it mixed-race families lack official recognition in Japan. In cases of international marriage, the foreign spouse appears as "missing" technically making the child illegitimate and the Japanese spouse a single-parent. Legally problems could and have happened when the Japanese spouse passes away and the children are officially classified as orphans. In cases of divorce foreign parents have had legal difficulties gaining child custody (BBC, 2003; Brophy 2003; Matusbara, 2003).

In 2011, in Shiki City just north of Tokyo, another seal "Ara-*chan*" made its temporary home near in the Arakawa River and become a local celebrity and media darling. "Ara-*chan*" did not attain the same lofty heights and fame as "Tama-*chan*" but he touched the hearts of Shiki residents and officials enough to be given a special resident permit because as a city official explained, "it has become a close friend to local people" (Reuters, 2011). Perhaps two fellow mammals brought the hypocrisy to light and effected change in Japanese bureaucratic policy because as of July 2012 foreign nationals residing in Japan are now registered in the *juminhyo*.

7. CONCLUSION

Japan, mainly due to its changing demographic structure, is a country facing many challenges to its social, economic, cultural and political systems. This book demonstrated how this demographic shift has led to increased immigration and tourism from a variety of countries and as a consequence international marriage involving diverse groups of foreigners with 'mainstream' Japanese has also increased. This, in turn, has led to greater numbers of a new minority group in Japan commonly referred to as *hafus* being born and raised in Japan.

This book focused on visibly mixed ethnic and cultural Japanese children and their parent's linguistic and cultural educational strategies. One of the main goals of this study was to see how and to what extent foreign parents taught their native language and culture to their children and what type of decisions are made for their children's education. A further aim of this study was to see the reasons why strategies or non-strategies are used by the parents and the effectiveness of these strategies in the setting of Japan.

Though there were some obvious limitations with this study regarding the age, ethnicity, cultural background, number of participants, the frequency and duration of the interviews, as well as the fact that most of the participant families lived in the same city; it is felt that despite these limitations a greater awareness of visibly mixed ethnic and cultural Japanese children living in Japan and their parent's educational strategies has been achieved.

Previous work has usually focused on young adults and their self-identity issues. In particular two specific groups of mixed ethnic and cultural Japanese have been studied; those that attend international schools and those who are the offspring of US military personnel and 'mainstream' Japanese parents, usually in Okinawa. These two groups offer very different perspectives of visibly mixed ethnic and cultural heritage Japanese living in

Japan. The international school group is in many ways one of privilege and possibilities due to the various forms of social, linguistic, and cultural capital they possess. The Okinawan group is usually portrayed as the other extreme because they often lack social, linguistic, and cultural capital and their story has often been one of abandonment and discrimination. In this sense, previous work has demonstrated the social realities of Japan during those times. That reality was that mixed ethnic and cultural Japanese in Japan lived on the edges of society usually the lower but also the upper extremes. More recent work though very scarce has shown a more balanced picture of mixed ethnic and cultural Japanese living in Japan.

This book has added onto previous work and it has expanded on the understanding of the experiences of mixed ethnic and cultural Japanese living in Japan today. This study looked mostly at younger elementary aged children attending regular Japanese public schools. These families living interspersed amongst the majority 'mainstream' Japanese population in a rather ordinary Japanese city has shed light on the changing social and ethno-cultural landscape of Japan today. This study has shown the middle way of life in Japan for mixed ethnic and cultural Japanese that perhaps was not possible in the past. This study, which explored how mixed ethnic and cultural families live their lives, can be seen as a microcosm of the social and cultural changes taking place in Japan today. Mixed ethnic and cultural families are choosing to live in various places throughout Japan and no longer live in isolated groups apart from 'mainstream' Japanese people and society.

The most striking aspect of this study was that both parents and children mostly seemed to feel that their lives in Japan today are quite 'normal'. Parents were mostly content with the Japanese education system, especially elementary school level education and felt no need to have their children attend an international school to avoid discrimination or to have a more multicultural school environment and education. In fact, the idea of their children learning about Japanese language and culture in Japan among Japanese peers was seen as a positive.

The older children in this study and a few of the younger ones did show an awareness of their dual nationalities and bicultural backgrounds but for the most part, the children felt that they were 'normal' Japanese. They had no major self-identity conflicts and had no feelings of being 'lost between worlds'. More than anyone it seemed if there was a sense of being an 'outsider' it was felt from the foreign parents and not the children. In some ways, these feelings expressed by the children is due to their young age but is also due to the overall acceptance by their peers and the communities they live in. This would seem to point to a more multicultural aware and accepting Japan today than in the past. This study has shown that various factors such as the ethnicity, cultural background, socio-economic class and gender of the foreign parent as they relate to Japan in the sense of time and place can change the perception and experiences of visibly mixed ethnic and cultural Japanese living in Japan. These children due to the widespread positive images of mixed ethnic and cultural Japanese in various media and professional sports in Japan today have an advantage in that the awareness and acceptance of mixed ethnic and cultural Japanese has become almost a matter of fact in Japanese society. This does not deny that cases of discrimination and bullying towards mixed ethnic and cultural Japanese can and does sometimes take place but points out that ethnic and cultural difference is more commonplace in Japan today than in the past.

In the coming years with further immigration, increasing tourism, continued international marriage and more mixed ethnic and cultural Japanese living in Japan questions about how the Japanese government will react to this changing cultural dynamic in Japanese society and what preparations will be made legally, economically, socially and educationally to ease this change will grow in importance.

The life experiences and stories of these children growing up in Japan are still in their early stages. These Japanese children are a part of Japan's cultural landscape, society, and future. By growing up in regular Japanese neighborhoods with 'mainstream' Japanese and visibly foreign parents and more importantly by attending regular public schools these children and their families are and will continue to be 'natural' agents of change and multiculturalism. Some of these children may not become completely bilingual and bicultural but their visibly mixed appearance will still do as much or more, from a grassroots level than any political rhetoric or even the best intentioned government policies, in achieving and creating awareness of ethnic and cultural diversity in Japan and in debunking any remnant notions of Japanese homogeneity.

Hafu is only a word but a word has power because it gives meaning and can create boundaries and set limitations by the scope of its commonly understood and acknowledged use. It is the hope of the parents that took part in this study that their children will not be limited by a word but that they will reach their full human potential.

HALF JAPANESE

BIBLIOGRAPHY

Arudou, D., (2004) JAPANESE ONLY: The Otaru Hotspring Case and Discrimination Against "Foreigners" in Japan. *The Asia-Pacific Journal: Japan Focus,* [online] Available at: <http://www.japanfocus.org/-Arudou-Debito/1743>

Arudou, D., (2007) Japan's Future as an International, Multicultural Society: From Migrants   Immigrants. *The Asia-Pacific Journal: Japan Focus,* [online] Available at: <http://www.japanfocus.org/-Arudou-Debito/2559>

Arudou, D., (2011) JUST BE CAUSE 'Sexlessness' wrecks marriages, threatens nation's future. *Japan Times Online,* [online] Available at: <http://search.japantimes.co.jp/cgi-bin/fl20110906ad.html>

BBC (2003) Japan seal slips through the net. *BBC news,* [online] Available at: <http://news.bbc.co.uk/2/hi/asia-pacific/2840083.stm>

Bourdieu, P., (1977) *Outline of a Theory of Practice.* Translated by R. Nice. Cambridge: Cambridge University Press.

Brasor, P., (2018) Japan is struggling to deal with the foreign tourism boom. *Japan Times Online,* [online] Available at: <https://www.japantimes.co.jp/news/2018/05/05/national/media-national/japan-struggling-deal-foreign-tourism-boom/#.W--rezFoTIV >

Brophy, B., (2003) Kawaii sea lion back in spotlight: Foreigners flip over Tama-chan's new status. *Japan Times Online,* [online] Available at: < https://www.japantimes.co.jp/community/2003/02/11/issues/kawaii-sea-lion-back-in-spotlight/#.W96r1TFoTIX >

Burgess, C., (2004) Discourses of Homogeneity in a Rapidly Globalizing Japan. *Electronic Journal of Contemporary Japanese Studies,* [online] Available at: <http://www.japanesestudies.org.uk/articles/Burgess.html>

Burgess, C., (2007) Multicultural Japan? Discourse and the 'Myth' of Homogeneity. *The Asia-Pacific Journal: Japan Focus,* [online] Available at: <http://www.japanfocus.org/-Chris-Burgess/2389>

Burgess, C., (2010) The 'Illusion' of Homogeneous Japan and National Character: Discourse as a Tool to Transcend the 'Myth' vs. 'Reality' Binary. *The Asia-Pacific Journal: Japan Focus,* [online] Available at: <http://www.japanfocus.org/-Chris-Burgess/3310>

Caryl, C. and Kashiwagi A., (2006) This is the New Japan: Immigrants are Transforming a Once Insular Society. *The Asia-Pacific Journal: Japan Focus,* [online] Available at: <http://www.japanfocus.org/-A-KASHIWAGI/2265>

CBS (2015) Beauty queen brings light to Japan's racial issues. *CBS This Morning* [online] Available at: https://www. cbsnews. Com /news /meet-ariana-miyamoto – first – biracial - miss-universe-japan/

Clark, G., (2005) Japan's Migration Conundrum. *The Asia-Pacific Journal: Japan Focus,* [online] Available at: <http://japanfocus.org/-/-Gregory-Clark/1727>

CNN (2018) Why are almost half of Japan's millennials still virgins? *CNN,* [online] Available at: <https://edition.cnn.com/2016/09/20/asia/japanese-millennials-virgins/index.html >

Creighton, M., (1997) Soto Others and uchi Others: imaging racial diversity, imagining homogeneous Japan. In Weiner, Michael (ed.) *Japan's Minorities: The Illusion of Homogeneity.* Oxon: Routledge.

Douglass, M. and Roberts, G.S., (2000) Japan in a global age of migration. In Douglass, Mike and Roberts, S. Glenda (eds.) *Japan and Global Migration: Foreign Workers and the Advent of a Multicultural Society.* Honolulu: Routledge.

Gluck, C., (1985) *Japan's Modern Myths: Ideology in the Late Meiji Period.* Princeton: Princeton University Press.

Graburn H.H. N., Ertl, J. and Tierney, K., (eds.) (2010) *Multiculturalism in the New Japan: Crossing the Boundaries Within.* New York: Berghan Books.

Graburn, N. and Ertl, J., (2010) Internal Boundaries and Models of Multiculturalism in Contemporary Japan. In Graburn H.H. Nelson, Ertl, John and Tierney, Kenji (eds.) *Multiculturalism in the New Japan: Crossing the Boundaries Within.* New York: Berghan Books.

Grenfell, E. ed., (2008) *Pierre Bourdieu: Key Concepts.* Durham: Acumen Publishing.

Hall, J.W., (1991) *Japan: From Prehistory to Modern Times.* Ann Arbor: The University of Michigan Center for Japanese Studies.

Hane, M, (2001) *Modern Japan: A Historical Survey.* Oxford: Westview Press.

Hisane, M., (2006) Japan Stares into a Demographic Abyss. *The Asia-Pacific Journal: Japan Focus,* [online] Available at: <http://www.japanfocus.org/-Hisane-MASAKI/1864>

Haub, C., (2010) Japan's Demographic Future. *Population Reference Bureau* [online] Available at: <https://www.prb.org/japandemography/>

Japan Times Online (2008) More children born with a foreign parent - Japan needs to deal with legal ramifications, experts say. *Japan Times Online,* [online] Available at: <http://search.japantimes.co.jp/cgi-bin/nn20080804a1.html>

Jardine, Lise (2012) International education a triple-An investment in your child's-and Japan's-future. *Japan Times Online,* [online] Available at: <http://www.japantimes.co.jp/text/fl20120110zg.html>

Kamada, L.D., (1995) Bilingual Family Case Studies (Vol. 1). Monographs on Bilingualism No.3. Tokyo: *Japan Association for Language Teaching,* Bilingualism SIG.

Kamada, L.D., (1997) Bilingual Family Case Studies (Vol. 2). Monographs on Bilingualism No.5. Tokyo: *Japan Association for Language Teaching,* Bilingualism SIG.

Kamada, L.D., (2010) *Hybrid Identities and Adolescent Girls: Being 'Half' in Japan.* Bristol: Multilingual Matters.

Kamata, S., (2009) Call Me Okaasan: An Introduction. In: S. Kamata (ed.) *Call Me Okaasan: Adventures in Multicultural Mothering.* Oregon: Wyatt-MacKenzie Publishing, Inc.

Kaneko, R. et al., (2008) Population Projections for Japan: 2006-2055 Outline of Results, Methods, and Assumptions, [pdf] *The Japanese Journal of Population* Vol.6, No.1. Available at: <http://www.ipss.go.jp/webj-ad/Webjournal.files/population/2008_4/05population.pdf>

Kelsky, K., (2001) *Women on the Verge: Japanese Women, Western Dreams,* London: Duke University Press.

Kingston, J., (2011) *Japan in Transformation 1945-2010,* Harlow: Pearson.

Kopf, D., (2018) The world is running out of Japanese people. *Quartz,* [online] Available at: <https://qz.com/1295721/the-japanese-population-is-shrinking-faster-than-every-other-big-country/>

Kyodo (2018) Japan looks to crack down on abuse of health insurance system as it plans for foreign worker influx. *Japan Times Online,* [online] Available   at: <https://www.japantimes.co.jp/news/2018/11/07/national/japans-health-insurance-overhaul-prevent-abuses-mainly-foreigners/#.W-gNFjFoTIV>

Large, S.S., (1997) *Emperors of the Rising Sun: Three Biographies,* Tokyo: Kodansha.

Lise, M.Y. and Willer, N.M., (2009) *The Hafu Project: Research, Photography and Interview Project,* [pdf] Available at: <www.hafuproject.com>

Mainichi Daily News (2010) Father of schoolgirl suicide victim says daughter was teased about mom's nationality. *The Mainichi Daily News,* [online] Available at: <http://mdn.mainichi.jp/mdnnews/national/news/20101027p2a00m0na0 07000c.html>

Matsubara, H., (2003) IN TAMA-CHAN'S WAKE: Foreigners seek same rights as seal. *Japan Times Online,* [online] Available at: <https://www.japantimes.co.jp/news/2003/02/23/national/foreigners-seek-same-rights-as-seal/#.W9mTuzFoTIV>

McNeill, D. et al., (2009) Lowering the Drawbridge of Fortress Japan: Citizenship, Nationality and the Rights of Children. *The Asia-Pacific Journal: Japan Focus,* [online] Available at: <http://www.japanfocus.org/-Hongo-Jun/3143>

Ministry of Justice (2010) *Basic Plan for Immigration Control* [pdf] Available at: <http://www.immi-moj.go.jp/seisaku/keikaku_101006_english.pdf>

Ministry of Justice (2015) *Basic Plan for Immigration Control* (5thEd.) [pdf] Available   at: <http://www.immi-moj.go.jp/seisaku/2015_kihonkeikaku_honbun_pamphlet_english.pdf>

Ministry of Health Labor and Welfare (1997) *On the Basic Viewpoint Regarding the Trend Towards Fewer Children - A Society of Decreasing Population: Responsibilities and Choices for the Future,* [online] Available at: <http://www1.mhlw.go.jp/english/council/c0126-2.html>

Ministry of Health Labor and Welfare (2009) Vital Statistics 2009. *Statistics and Information Department,* [Exl] Table 1-37 Number of marriages by nationality of husband and wife, by year, [online] Available at <http://www.mhlw.go.jp/english/database/db-hh/xls/1-37.xls>

Ministry of Internal Affairs and Communications, (2018a) Statistical Handbook of Japan 2018, *Statistics Bureau, Ministry of Internal Affairs and Communications, Japan* [online] Available at <https://www.stat.go.jp/data/jinsui/pdf/201810.pdf>

Ministry of Internal Affairs and Communications, (2018) Statistical Handbook of Japan 2018, *Statistics Bureau, Ministry of Internal Affairs and Communications, Japan* [online] Available at <https://www.stat.go.jp/english/data/handbook/pdf/2018all.pdf#page=17>

Morris-Suzuki, T., (1998) *Re-inventing Japan: time, space, nation.* New York: M E Sharpe Inc.

Morris-Suzuki, T., (2002) Immigration and citizenship in contemporary Japan. In Maswood, J. Graham, J. and Miyajima, H. (eds.) *Japan – change and continuity,* 163-178, Routledge Curzon & Copy.

Murphy-Shigematsu, S., (2000) *The Voices of Amerasians: Ethnicity, Identity, and Empowerment in Interracial Japanese Americans.* USA: Dissertation.com.

Murphy-Shigematsu, S., (2001) Multiethnic Lives and Monoethnic Myths: American-Japanese Amerasians in Japan. *Multicultural Leadership,* [online] Available at: <http://www.multiculturalleadership.com/essays.htm>

Murphy-Shigematsu, S., (2002) Multicultural Encounters: Case Narratives from a Counseling Practice. New York: Teachers College Press.

Murphy-Shigematsu, S., (2008) The invisible man and other narratives of living in the borderlands of race and nation. In: D.B. Willis and S. Murphy-Shigematsu (eds.) *Transcultural Japan: At the borderlands of race, gender, and identity.* Oxon: Routledge.

Neary, I., (1997) Burakumin in contemporary Japan. In: Weiner, Michael (ed.) *Japan's Minorities: the Illusion of Homogeneity.* Oxon: Routledge.

Nippon Communications Foundation, (2017) Japan's Annual Births Drop Below 1 Million: 2016 Demographic Statistics. *nippon.com,* [online] Available at: <https://www.nippon.com/en/features/h00160/>

Noiri, N., (2011) Schooling and identity in Okinawa. In: R. Tsuneyoshi, K.H., Okano and S.S., Boocock (eds.) *Minorities and Education in Multicultural Japan,* Oxon: Routledge.

Nonomiya, L. and Oda, S., (2016) Blogger's viral tirade on day care puts Abe on back foot. *The Japan Times,* [online] Available at: <https://www.japantimes.co.jp/news/2016/03/15/national/social-issues/bloggers-die-japan-day-care-tirade-puts-abe-back-foot/#.W-ehrTFoTIV>

Okano, K. and Tsuneyoshi, R., (2011) Understanding minorities and education. In R. Tsuneyoshi, K.H., Okano and S.S., Boocock (eds.) *Minorities and Education in Multicultural Japan.* Oxon: Routledge.

Reuters (2011) Wandering seal a welcome relief for nervous Japanese. *Reuters,* [online] Available at: <https://www.reuters.com/article/japan-seal/wandering-seal-a-welcome-relief-for-nervous-japanese->

Roth, J., (2005) Political and Cultural Perspectives on Japan's Insider Minorities. *The Asia-Pacific Journal: Japan Focus,* [online] Available at: <http://www.japanfocus.org/-Joshua-Roth/1723>

Saberi, R., (2015) Being 'hafu' in Japan: Mixed-race people face ridicule, rejection.
Al Jazeera America News, [online] Available at: <http://america.aljazeera.com/articles/2015/9/9/hafu-in-japan-mixed-race.html>

Sakanaka, H., (2005) The Future of Japan's Immigration Policy: a battle diary. *The Asia-Pacific Journal: Japan Focus,* [online] Available at: <http://www.japanfocus.org/-Sakanaka-Hidenori/2396>

Sellek, Y., (1997) Nikkeijin: the phenomenon of return migration. In: Weiner, Michael (ed.) *Japan's Minorities: the Illusion of Homogeneity.* Oxon: Routledge.

Siddle, R., (1997) Ainu: Japan's indigenous people. In: Weiner, Michael (ed.) *Japan's Minorities: the Illusion of Homogeneity.* Oxon: Routledge.

Serio, K., (2015) Miss Universe: Half-Black Miss Japan Criticized for Not Being 'Japanese Enough'. *Breitbart.com.* [online] Available at: <https://www.breitbart.com/entertainment/2015/03/23/miss-universe-half-black-miss-japan-criticized-for-not-being-japanese-enough/>

Siddle, R., (2008) *Race and Identity in Modern Japan.* University of Sheffield, unpublished ms.

Taira, K., (1997) Troubled national identity: the Ryukyuans/Okinawans. In: Weiner, Michael (ed.) *Japan's Minorities: the Illusion of Homogeneity.* Oxon: Routledge.

Tsuneyoshi, R., (2011) The Cultural Diversification in Education. In R. Tsuneyoshi, K.H., Okano and S.S., Boocock (eds.) *Minorities and Education in Multicultural Japan.* Oxon: Routledge.

United Nations (2009) World Population Prospects: The 2008 Revision, [pdf] New York: *United Nations, Department of Economic and Social Affairs, Population Division,* Available at: <http://www.un.org/esa/population/publications/wpp2008/wpp2008_highlights.pdf>

United Nations (2011) World Population Prospects, The 2010 Revision, [online] New York: *United Nations, Department of Economic and Social Affairs, Population Division,* Available at: <http://esa.un.org/unpd/wpp/index.htm>

United Nations (2017) World Population Prospects, The 2010 Revision, [online] New York: *United Nations, Department of Economic and Social Affairs, Population Division,* Available at: <https://population.un.org/wpp/Download/Standard/Population/>

United Nations (2010) World Population Ageing 2009, [pdf] New York: *United Nations, Department of Economic and Social Affairs, Population Division,* Available at: <http://www.un.org/esa/population/publications/WPA2009/WPA2009_WorkingPaper.pdf>

United Nations (2010a) World Fertility Report: 2007, [pdf] New York: *United Nations, Department of Economic and Social Affairs, Population Division,* Available at: <http://www.un.org/esa/population/publications/worldfertilityreport200 7/wfr2007-text.pdf>

Vasishth, A., (1997) A model minority: the Chinese community in Japan. In: Weiner, Michael (ed.) *Japan's Minorities: the Illusion of Homogeneity.* Oxon: Routledge.

Wakatsuki, Y., and Griffiths, J., (2018) Number of children in Japan shrinks to new record low. *CNN,* [online] Available at: <https://edition.cnn.com/2018/05/07/health/japan-child-population-record-low-intl/index.html>

Weiner, M., (1997) The representation of absence and the absence of representation: Korean victims of the atomic bomb. In: Weiner, Michael (ed.) *Japan's Minorities: the Illusion of Homogeneity.* Oxon: Routledge.

Weiner, M. (1997) *Japan's Minorities: The Illusion of Homogeneity.* Oxon, Routledge.

Willis, D.B., (2001) Pacific Creoles: The Power of Hybridity in Japanese-American Relations. In: T. Matsuda (ed.) *The Age of Creolization in the Pacific: In Search of Emerging Cultures and Shared Values in the Japan-America Borderlands.* Hiroshima: Keisuisha.

Willis, D.B., (2008) Dejima: creolization and enclaves of difference in transnational Japan. In: D.B. Willis and S. Murphy-Shigematsu (eds.) *Transcultural Japan: At the borderlands of race, gender, and identity.* Oxon: Routledge.

Yamawaki, K., (2000) Foreign workers in Japan: a historical perspective. In Douglass, Mike and Roberts, S. Glenda (eds.) *Japan and Global Migration: Foreign Workers and the Advent of a Multicultural Society.* Honolulu: Routledge.

Yoshino, K., (1992) The Nihonjinron: thinking elites' ideas of Japanese uniqueness. Yoshino, Kosaku, *Cultural nationalism in contemporary Japan: a sociological enquiry,* 9-38,228-232, Routledge & copy; <http://www.tandf.co.uk/journals>

ABOUT THE AUTHOR

Timothy Dooley was born in Montreal, Canada. He came to Japan in 1998; originally on a working holiday visa with the intention of staying a few months before traveling to other parts of Asia and heading home to a career in teaching. Enjoying Japan and meeting his wife, with whom he has two children, led to him staying longer than he expected. He has a B.A., B.Ed., and an M.A. He is a teacher and writer living in Osaka, Japan.